THE
CRUX OF CARE
MANAGEMENT

THE
CRUX OF CARE
MANAGEMENT

*Steps to **Managed Care** and **Patient-Centric Service Excellence** for Leaders*

TRAMICO **HERMAN**

Published by Advantage, Charleston, South Carolina.
Member of Advantage Media Group.

ADVANTAGE is a registered trademark, and the Advantage colophon is a trademark of Advantage Media Group, Inc.

Printed in the United States of America.

10 9 8 7 6 5 4 3 2 1

ISBN: 978-1-64225-306-1
LCCN: 2021924779

Cover design by Analisa Smith.
Layout design by Wesley Strickland.

This publication is designed to provide accurate and authoritative information in regard to the subject matter covered. It is sold with the understanding that the publisher is not engaged in rendering legal, accounting, or other professional services. If legal advice or other expert assistance is required, the services of a competent professional person should be sought.

Advantage Media Group is proud to be a part of the Tree Neutral® program. Tree Neutral offsets the number of trees consumed in the production and printing of this book by taking proactive steps such as planting trees in direct proportion to the number of trees used to print books. To learn more about Tree Neutral, please visit www.treeneutral.com.

Advantage Media Group is a publisher of business, self-improvement, and professional development books and online learning. We help entrepreneurs, business leaders, and professionals share their Stories, Passion, and Knowledge to help others Learn & Grow. Do you have a manuscript or book idea that you would like us to consider for publishing? Please visit advantagefamily.com.

Contents

Acknowledgments

I wish to thank the following people for their contributions to my inspiration and knowledge and other help in my journey:

Raquel Sulal for your tremendous support and championing my efforts throughout the entire development of this book.

Dr. Jua'Nese Williams—my mentor, industry expert, and universal leader—for your unwavering support, insights, and recommendations, ensuring the importance of patient-centered care and compliance is conveyed.

Introduction

"Who knows what they want to be when they grow up?" My hand bolted skyward before the teacher finished asking the question. It was sixth-grade career day, and I couldn't wait to make my announcement. *Pick me! Pick me!* I nearly bounced from my little desk chair, vying for her attention, and it worked. Any student who wanted to could go to the front and share their career ambitions with the class. She called on me, and I had to stop myself from running up there.

"I want to be a nurse. I like to help people, and it makes me feel good, and I like to see a smile on someone's face." It's a time-honored tradition for little kids to proclaim grand aspirations for adulthood—everything from teacher to superhero is bandied about—but not many sixth graders stick to their proverbial guns and follow through. Ask me today, and I'll tell you that I built on that passion to help people in our community, our patients, make informed decisions and gain better control in regard to access to and quality of healthcare.

The motivation started at home. My younger sister has cerebral palsy, and at a very young age, I had to step up and help my mom and brothers take care of her. She had a feeding tube from her nose into her stomach that funneled nutrition through a syringe to feed her, and low oxygen levels were always a risk. Her fingertips and lips became warning signs; if they started turning a purplish color, it was time to connect the nasal cannula with oxygen. We knew that was the way she would survive, and when I saw her smile and thrive with what we provided, it warmed my heart and inspired an overwhelming feeling of love. Even as just a young kid, I knew it would be amazing to do that for other people as well.

As an African American growing up in metropolitan Cleveland, Ohio, living among other African Americans, Croatians, Arabs, Latinos, and Jews, my own community provided that opportunity. We lived in a place way down the socioeconomic ladder with a lack of resources across the board and a general knowledge deficit in things like healthcare. As I grew up, I noticed that many people struggled with illnesses that destroyed their lives and families; they couldn't work and couldn't provide, and it made the socioeconomic situation worse. We didn't have the same access to healthcare as other thriving neighborhoods—hospitals were run down, ERs didn't have adequate staff, and sanitation was poor. It really bothered me, and it wasn't just broken bones or diabetes treatment; mental illnesses like schizophrenia and bipolar disorder were prevalent as well, with little acceptance, understanding, or even recognition of the issue. There's a disconnect in fully understanding how the brain works, and in fact, individuals in my culture with mental or behavioral health conditions are often outcast without guidance or support. They self-medicate with drugs, alcohol, and other unhealthy choices.

It goes back to a lack of education and trust in the healthcare system, where the psychosocial is ignored more than the physical. We can't choose our families or their financial status, but we need an equal playing field, and I wanted to be on the front line to speak my voice and do whatever I could to support equal healthcare treatment, to bridge that gap to empowerment and community support.

In my high school honors program at age seventeen, I didn't have a lot of classes during my senior year and enrolled in our vocational option with a half day in school and half working as a nursing assistant at a local nursing home. Along with traditional healthcare scenarios, I saw consistent substandard treatment of the elderly, and still today we don't embrace aging and tend to see that population as an annoyance and herd them into extended care facilities and forget about them. But when you're there and see them depressed and deprived of a family unit, the familiarity of home, and connection to community, the problem is glaringly clear. This population is suffering, and these are the people who laid the foundation; we can't just shut them out because they don't move as fast as they used to or their minds don't respond in a heartbeat. When I became part of the healthcare environment, I made sure to take time with the elderly and listen to their stories no matter how many times they repeated them, and if they didn't have family members near, I wanted to be there. I have a special place in my heart for the elderly, whether they are part of extended care facilities or my neighbors.

What does this all mean for you? In a word, understanding. The main goal of health plan care management programs is to help patients, or "members" in industry parlance, understand their conditions, whether they have diabetes, high blood pressure, high cholesterol, or dementia. We build from there with comprehension of learning gaps. For example, maybe a member doesn't understand the association of nutrition with health and how they should be eating or managing specific medications. Why is that important? What is the optimal time to take your blood pressure? We work collectively with teams of nurses, physicians, respiratory therapists, pharmacists, and social workers to help members understand what's going on with their health and provide actionable education.

The core of our care management programs is to help healthcare teams operate like centers of excellence through training, guidance, mentoring, and accountability to help members through the healthcare process. We advocate for them and spend a lot of time with hospitals, doctors' offices, outpatient centers, and community organizations to best utilize all tools and all opportunities. This book will help internal program leaders assess their needs, foster growth, and improve operations, resulting in profitability, quality member service, and overall healthcare system excellence.

I am fortunate to have had the opportunity to leverage my childhood passion into a place of giving back and making a difference. I began my nursing career leading hospital medical/surgical and intensive care units as a charge nurse, providing care and executing physician care plans to multiple complex patients, heading teams of nurses, unit clerks, and nursing assistants. After five years of working in hospitals, I evaluated my career and decided I wanted to operate in a different atmosphere. I had the opportunity to collaborate with leaders who worked for leading pharmaceutical, healthcare insurance, and public health organizations. With that exposure to managed care, I knew there was more for me, so I leveraged their guidance and transitioned to healthcare administration with a focus on care management, utilization management, and population health.

In a role at a large health plan as a frontline care manager/utilization review nurse, I provided education and care coordination to members, helping them move to healthier lifestyles while decreasing their overall healthcare utilization spending. Later I advanced to leadership roles as team lead and project manager, enhancing operations, managing staff performance, developing strategies for process improvements, reducing employee turnover, and supporting recruitment and quality compliance with executive leaders. I eventually earned an MBA with a project management concentration and decided that, after working for a large health plan for seven years with successful progression, it was time to transition to consulting based on my mentor recommendations. From there I further advanced my business/clinical skills, supporting various Fortune 100 health plans and providers serving in director, senior project manager, manager, and principal consultant roles in leading care management transformations.

I am passionate about healthcare and continue working hard to improve my skills in closing some of the most critical gaps impacting our communities' access to and quality of care. I have been blessed thus far that my journey has positively impacted my immediate family and friends through mentoring and guidance. Professionally I've had the opportunity to train thousands of staff on effective operations and role execution, improve millions of members' lives related to improved care management program delivery, and help clients save over $50 million of lost revenue. This is my space and my place to drive change.

In the pages ahead, I share a step-by-step approach to care management, from self-awareness and industry expertise to team autonomy and process improvement. We'll dive into the crux of care management, walking through a member's journey of the managed care healthcare continuum and understanding what should happen and what is not happening.

CHAPTER 1

Attain Self-Awareness

It's surprising how many persons go through life without ever recognizing that their feelings toward other people are largely determined by their feelings toward themselves, and if you're not comfortable within yourself, you can't be comfortable with others.

—SYDNEY J. HARRIS

I n 2006 it became apparent that I needed to take the advice I gave many of my patients, to speak with a personal development coach to understand who I am and the impact of my behaviors. I was concerned about emotions I experienced at the time, the effect it would have on my health, and how I treated others. After accepting that I needed help, I began working with a coach who taught me about the interrelationships of the mind—feelings and behavior influenced by many variables during human developmental stages. The most valuable information I learned was how my upbringing significantly influenced my view of the world and decisions about my life. Some things were beneficial, while others were not, but I learned how to move beyond biases, judgment, resistance, and mismanagement of my ego. This was a major turning point in my life and continues to guide my thoughts and behaviors with family, friends, professionals, work team members, and patients. Now I am able to do a pulse check and apply healthy reasoning before responding to any situation.

It really helped me understand why I was doing what I was doing and was so important in recognizing that there were opportunities for me to change—for example, becoming easily irritated or not having control of my temperament or being impatient in certain situations. It was critical to know that I had those types of traits, and I needed to address that and come up with positive ways of managing them. If I'm in a challenging situation, I already have a game plan and know how to deal with it versus reacting with outbursts or retaliating and damaging a relationship with a peer or team member. I had the tools—a combination of reading, meditation, and other avenues—to get me back into a balanced and harmonious state.

What It Means to Have Self-Awareness

Self-awareness is the foundation, the pathway. It is the essence of emotional intelligence that allows you to observe your mind, behavior, and feelings as an outsider to evaluate who you are. If you don't know who you are as a person, that crosses over into your personal and professional lives and creates a disconnect between what you stand for and your principles and values. This deep reflection allows you to understand how family influences who you think you are, how you treat others, what you believe about others, how to conduct yourself, how to manage relationships with them and others, and how to manage career choices.

Self-awareness also inspires understanding of your personality type to discover your work style and how you can best contribute to your organization. For example, according to the Myers-Briggs personality indicator, I am what they call and ESTJ type—extroverted, sensing, thinking, judging. *Extroverts* are energized by time spent with others and prefer to focus on the outside world. *Sensing* focuses on fact and details rather than concepts. *Thinking* refers to decisions based on logical consequences of actions. *Judging* prefers structure and organization rather than being spontaneous and flexible. Having this insight allows you to understand your work style in five distinct ways:

If you don't know who you are as a person, that crosses over into your personal and professional lives and creates a disconnect between what you stand for and your principles and values.

1. **Improve communication and teamwork as you gain awareness of personality differences you see in others.** Knowing others' preferences allows you to develop strategies to more effectively deliver information and work within personal interactions. For example, if I am working with an ESTJ like myself, I would be aware this team member is more receptive to concrete, specific facts and details relevant to the task at hand with defined goals and priorities that are realistic, clear, and specific. The person of this style may also become impatient with long discussions, cut people off, and not give all team members a chance to contribute. In this case you would coach the individual to be patient and hear out each team member for his or her ideas and reflect what was heard. This is also an ideal time to share with team members your communication preferences to accurately retrieve information related to their tasks, performance, concerns, and

ideas. If someone learns a little slower, it doesn't mean they're incompetent; there's just a different learning style. If someone doesn't speak up, it doesn't mean they don't understand; they could be uncomfortable in large groups. It really goes into knowing who you are, and that will be your strength and the ability to make sure you are treating your team with purposeful thought, avoiding conflict, and leaving a good impression on the people you work with. To fully connect with a team, you have to connect with everyone on it.

2. **Work more effectively with those who may approach problems and decisions very differently from how you do.** This includes showing compassion and consideration for all personality types and creating an all-inclusive environment. In addition to understanding how team members process, react to, and execute information related to trainings, policies, and workflows, you can help them optimize their strengths while supporting growth in areas of opportunities. For example, the ESTJ type leans to methodical, logical approaches based on facts, so they may be resistant to adopting a theoretical approach that will benefit work delivery. This is a perfect time to bring clarity and explain the benefits of considering both practical and theoretical concepts.

3. **Navigate your work and personal relationships with more insight and effectiveness.** Making purposeful decisions considering all factors allows you to function as your best self while managing teams through various complex activities, guiding family through difficult moments, and supporting friends in times of need.

4. **Understand your preferences for learning and work environments and the activities and work you most enjoy doing.** This allows you to be fulfilled in your role and perform your duties with efficiency and pride. Happiness at the workplace equates to higher productivity. When you feel good about what you're doing, when you're able to work in a way that you most relate to and people understand you, it creates a feeling of joy and happiness. And we all know that when you feel good inside and fulfilled, productivity is higher.

5. **More successfully manage the everyday conflicts and stresses that work and life may bring.** It is important to know your conflict management strengths to resolve sensitive matters with professionalism, compassion, and accuracy. This eliminates major issues and brings a sense of calm to your team, allowing them to move forward with work activities. It is just as critical to know potential challenges you may face related to your conflict style to avoid making team members feel uncomfortable, not valued, or not understood, which could lead to disruption. For example, ESTJ types can sometimes be overpowering, particularly in a conflict situation, and want to move things along quickly and may appear noncaring. This would be a time to slow down and avoid making immediate decisions. It is also important to know stressors, including

   ➡ not having control of your own time and schedule;

   ➡ dealing with others' bad decisions;

   ➡ being personally attacked or unjustly criticized;

   ➡ being in a disorganized, chaotic environment; and

➡ coping with constantly changing goals and procedures.

None of us is perfect, and we face constant challenges. As a health-care professional, the end goal is having insight into workday needs and managing stressors appropriately without negatively impacting team members.

Orchestrating Life's Puzzle Pieces

When you've filled your personality bucket with an understanding of who you are, it sets the stage for learning how the brain leverages self-awareness to solve your own puzzle, see the missing pieces, and methodically put them back in place. What do I mean by that? My example of working with a personal development coach to understand life stages allowed me to eventually observe my mind and recognize the correlation between brain anatomy and its functions. With no impairment, human feelings and emotions coalesce in a smoothly functioning process. But nobody is perfect, and what happens when the brain isn't functioning at its optimal level?

Dopamine levels, for instance, are naturally wired to maintain a particular level, but when they decrease, depression sets in. The ways you normally feel, think, and behave are now distorted. Some deficiencies like this originate genetically, while others derive from external factors such as trauma in childhood or other points in your life. Understanding this process helps you put the pieces back together and function at a high level.

On the other hand, lack of understanding affects many behaviors, such as how you treat others and how you treat yourself, and that puts you at a disadvantage of an unfulfilled life, irrational behaviors, and ultimately a reactionary personality wrapped in a big ball of emotions.

Naturally that has a tremendous impact on your role in family, friendships, career, and everything else that makes up your world.

Remember that everything we learn initially comes from our parents. If we have siblings, it expands from there, but our first exposure to understanding what the world is all about is based on what they tell us and show us. Consider the hierarchy and definitions of the roles of parents, children, nieces, and nephews and the expectations of those roles. It all plays a part in how you perceive and interact with others. We are generally taught to respect our parents and siblings and grow up with a particular ideal. In relationships outside of family, you already have a foundation, a picture in your mind, of how others might engage with their parents or siblings. This becomes very important when encountering scenarios that don't match your outlook or personality. You have expectations of how things should work, and when they don't, you want to correct them.

It's very important to recognize the role you play and understand that people are different. Being open and willing to learn other cultures brings it all together and makes you happy.

BENEFITS OF SELF-AWARENESS

In a leadership role, understanding traditional human developmental stages helps you avoid bias and prejudice. Complemented with a full awareness of your personality type, it allows you to function at an optimal level, make fair decisions, and develop unique communication strategies for your team. Based on their personality types, you can effectively manage conflict, reduce stress levels and outbursts, and build trusting relationships in a calm and cohesive work environment. In addition, being attuned to self-awareness allows you to authentically connect with and empathize with health plan members, taking accountability as an advocate to ensure everything is done right throughout the member healthcare continuum.

CONSEQUENCES OF A LACK OF SELF-AWARENESS

A lack of self-awareness opens up a slew of challenges and potentially life-changing outcomes. In short if you don't understand human development, cultures, and other races, it will almost always result in unfair treatment and harm to others. Lack of understanding your personality type adds a litany of additional struggles:

- Functioning at substandard level, making poor decisions
- Ineffective communication, leading to confusion and meager work execution
- Hostility from poorly managed conflict
- High stress levels, affecting the health of yourself and your team
- Chaotic work environment
- Damaged relationships

BEGIN BY

What steps are required to develop robust self-awareness?

- Start by scheduling a few sessions with a personal development coach and obtain a psychometric assessment.
- Take a leading personality test like the Myers-Briggs indicator to determine your strengths and gifts to give to others and then apply those recommendations.

- Read emotional intelligence books, journals, and articles and participate in webinars and trainings.

- Participate in self-care like meditation, work-life balance, exercise, and healthy nutrition.

- Don't take life too seriously; embrace humor to balance emotions and bring harmony.

Remember, self-awareness is the foundation to understanding your true self while eliminating false narratives learned from external factors and your mind. It is critical to participate in activities to initiate and maintain awareness to improve decision-making abilities and balance your emotions, resulting in high performance, compassion for others, achieving your goals, and ultimate gratification. Be your best you!

Now that you understand who you are and how to use your strengths and gifts to optimize your contributions in work settings, you are ready to take real steps to evolve to the next phase of leadership: an industry expert.

CHAPTER 2

Become an Industry Expert

A leader is one who knows the way, goes the way, and shows the way.

—KEITH LAU

A client vision session changed my career. During my tenure at a top four consulting firm, I attended what is essentially a meeting of the minds where executive leaders and directors gathered to uncover what's working well and what isn't. We assessed a care management program to determine leading practice recommendations, and my managing director, Marjorie Bogaert, delivered a powerful message. An industry stalwart for nearly forty years, Marjorie has worked in multiple hospital settings and for a top consulting firm. On this day she provided a thorough overview of care management operations, its role in health plan and provider organizations, and the financial impact if not managed appropriately.

It was apparent that her confidence and expertise stemmed from years of experience in frontline, middle management, and executive leadership roles across various healthcare organizations. She delivered succinct answers to scenarios of moderate to high complexity to several of our client stakeholders. It can be challenging introducing new ideas and eliciting engagement to an organization accustomed to performing their work with a model used for years. Marjorie empathized with their concerns but continued to share leading practice findings supported by other client case studies, white papers, articles, and guiding principles, convincing them that her recommended changes were a tall order but necessary to improve patient safety and increase profitability. I left the session with a new level of respect for her and told myself I wanted to deliver solutions just like that.

Care management departments are some of the most, if not the most, important departments of a hospital and health plans. Everything else depends on it, and Marjorie fielded every inquiry, even the highly charged, with confident grace as she discussed how new recommendations would improve operations. I had already admired her work, but this event brought it to another level. We were already working together, and she took me under her wing as a mentor and showed me how to become and showcase myself as an industry expert. "You have expertise already from skills you gained as a hospital charge nurse, care manager, health plan leader, project manager, and now consulting," she said. "You are one of my strongest team members."

It was a huge confidence boost, and our strong assessment findings and recommendations won the implementation, leading to our project team launching a very complex two-year project that further augmented my care management expertise in managing C-suite executive leaders. I moved from behind the scenes to front and center, leading steering committee meetings and staff. Marjorie's expectations were high, and she wanted things done a certain way, but she offered constructive feedback that shone a light on my work. By sharing her expert tools and confidence, I became an expert as well.

By sharing her expert tools and confidence, I became an expert as well.

What It Means to Be an Industry Expert

Leadership doesn't start from the top; it starts from the bottom. Leaders are (or are expected to be) experts in their fields, but great leaders are not born as such; they ascend in knowledge and skill from their earliest days on the job, and that takes resourceful determination. When you eventually reach a leadership role, you want to continue that trajectory with the familiarity of accurate information and follow guiding principles, leading practice methodologies, and industry recommendations. The leadership space isn't the time or place for guessing; it is imperative to continue your education by participating in ongoing training for compliance updates, new medical treatments, technology advancements, current trends, and issue resolution. Your experience, of course, plays a big role, and you will lean on it often, but it still must map back to industry standard.

It is also important to collaborate with other industry experts, like executive leaders directing care management programs from other health plans, medical/business consultants, information technology gurus, human resource, and compliance leaders to learn and share best practices. This level of engagement/accountability positions you to move your organization to function as a center of excellence, using best practices to develop and support critical capabilities that align with organizational priorities—for example, member safety, high-quality services, profitability, sustainability, and growth.

And never stop learning. Continuing education should remain a high priority at all levels of growth. Nurses, for example, must maintain continuing education credits to keep their licenses active, a critical career requirement in a complex, highly regulated field forever changing in so many ways, including patients who are living longer with multiple conditions. An eighty-year-old patient might have coronary artery disease, high blood pressure, and Parkinson's, and they've had a stroke and a few other maladies. As such, treatment plans also evolve, doctors utilize different approaches to care, new drugs are released all the time, and of course technology changes constantly.

Continuing education should remain a high priority at all levels of growth.

Complementing continuing education is the invaluable benefit of collaborating with other experts. When I was with Blue Cross Blue Shield, I didn't limit myself to working only within that arena; I collaborated with people from other health plans as well. There is an incredible wealth of talent in healthcare; maybe a colleague across town is more aligned with leading practices or operates with an innovative, new approach. One organization doesn't have everything, and you need to cover the full spectrum if you're working to get your organization up to speed. A well-trained staff is priceless, but you need an internal engine precisely lined up with care management compliance standards.

Another valuable resource is consultants, experts in their specialty with years of targeted experience and, often, roles as directors or executive positions with healthcare insurance companies or hospitals. Traditionally they travel throughout a region or across the country, gleaning actionable knowledge and solutions with immediate application potential. Collaborating with them keeps you abreast of available resources that can drastically improve your own expertise and your organization as a whole. It allows efficient communication with the right people and inspires further collaboration with peers, managers, and frontline staff. Remember, however, that the best results start with one essential ingredient—you. Like any endeavor, quality in is quality out.

Do It Right When No One Is Looking

Henry Ford had a legendary work ethic and a penchant for quality. One of his most influential quotes is "Quality means doing it right when no one is looking." Henry was right; becoming an industry expert begins when you accept responsibility for your actions without a push from your direct supervisor, commit to providing high-quality service, contribute to an organization's vision, and influence others' actions to move in the direction you are going. Keep in mind that leadership doesn't typically start with a leadership role. For me I started thinking like an expert during my first healthcare role as a nursing assistant at age seventeen. When I was in a patient's room, providing care, no one else was there watching. Specific procedures must be followed, and it's up to the nurse to ensure that happens. With my passion for caring for people, I vowed from day one to provide fair, safe, and high-quality treatment to every patient. No one was in the room showing me step-by-step what to do, and I wasn't even old enough to be in a leadership position; I built on passion, natural and learned skills, and a drive to improve.

Some people are natural leaders, but your abilities expand from an array of personal and professional experiences. Every role you work contributes to your knowledge and performance. As you move to becoming a care management expert, it is imperative to understand required care coordination and system integration within the member journey through the healthcare continuum. Personally it took me a while because I really had to think about it from a compliance standard point of view, and with my focus today on health plans, I had to consider the three main regulatory agencies: National Committee for Quality Assurance (NCQA), Utilization Review Accreditation

Commission (URAC), and the Centers for Medicare and Medicaid Services (CMS). Policies and mandates from these regulatory agencies guide care management operations, which ultimately decide the trajectory of a member's care journey, whether it be an everyday doctor visit, an emergency room procedure, or a hospital admission.

These are fundamentals that tie into policies and workflows that are in an almost constant state of change. For example, regulatory agencies release updates every year, and as a leader, you need to keep pace and determine which operational tasks currently in play need to be eliminated or enhanced. Your organization likely has a compliance department, but you can't blindly trust that department; your understanding of the fundamentals defines everything. A failed regulatory audit can shut down a health insurance organization or suspend its ability to market its product. With billions of dollars at stake, compliance is king.

In that regard we will examine the following eleven phases of the member journey when requesting planned or unplanned services. Reference the case study in the upcoming section to walk through activities of the member, health plan (HP), and provider during each phase; procedural requirements based on regulatory agency standards (what's happening); and common opportunities (what's not happening) faced by many HPs. These opportunities are areas where modifications are required to align with procedural mandates ensuring compliance and healthy member outcomes.

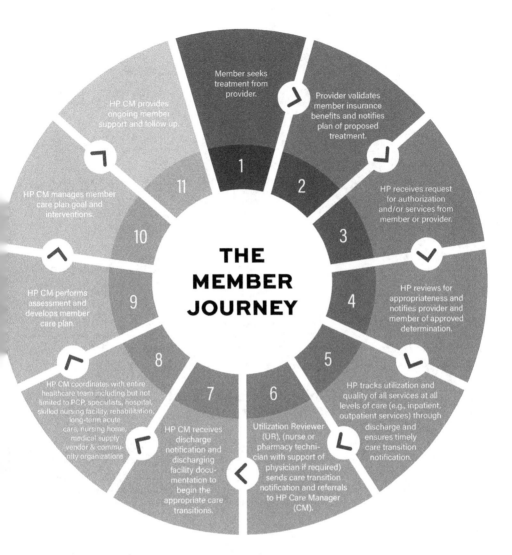

THE MEMBER JOURNEY

1. Member seeks treatment from provider.

2. Provider validates member insurance benefits and notifies plan of proposed treatment.

3. HP receives request for authorization and/or services from member or provider.

4. HP reviews for appropriateness and notifies provider and member of approved determination.

5. HP tracks utilization and quality of all services at all levels of care (e.g., inpatient, outpatient services) through discharge and ensures timely care transition notification.

6. Utilization Reviewer (UR), (nurse or pharmacy technician with support of physician if required) sends care transition notification and referrals to HP Care Manager (CM).

7. HP CM receives discharge notification and discharging facility documentation to begin the appropriate care transitions.

8. HP CM coordinates with entire healthcare team including but not limited to PCP, specialists, hospital, skilled nursing facility, rehabilitation, long-term acute care, nursing home, medical supply vendor & community organizations

9. HP CM performs assessment and develops member care plan.

10. HP CM manages member care plan goal and interventions.

11. HP CM provides ongoing member support and follow up.

Let's start with a member scenario. Put your expertise to work as you identify opportunities to improve the member experience and health outcomes.

Presentation

A seventy-five-year-old male enrolled in Medicare/Medicaid plan. Suffers from chest pain, shortness of breath (SOB), fatigue, history of coronary artery disease (CAD), hypertension, diabetes, gout, leg cramps, and muscle tenderness. He had three previous PCP visits over the past year regarding his complaints with no improvement."

Examination

The physical exam showed elevated BP (180/110), increased heart rate (HR) (130), sweating, and abnormal heart sounds. The PCP called EMS and had the member transported to the nearest hospital for emergency stabilization and management.

ER Stabilization to Hospital Admission

Arrived via ambulance with elevated blood pressure and heart rate and abnormal EKG. Placed on telemetry with three liters of oxygen (O2), blood sugar (BS) of 400, and positive troponin levels. Admitted with a diagnosis (Dx) of atherosclerotic heart disease with one blocked artery and unstable angina to progressive care unit (PCU). Financial services called the after-hours number for the UM department to obtain authorization number. HP after-hours was limited to discharge coordination of care only; the HP was closed until Monday.

Initial Review and Retrospective Review of Weekend

Monday afternoon (hospital day 3). ADT indicated member admission to a nonparticipating out-of-network (OON) hospital and summarized the following: "Patient remained stable with no further chest pain, SOB, BS range 88–120, BP range 110/72 to 122/78, normal sinus rhythm (NSR), and planned for cardiac catheterization today." Did not meet guidelines for acute inpatient. Observation care only. The case was approved for inpatient admission and to continue with daily concurrent review until discharge. Care management system lacks the ability to automate data retrieval from OON providers or send payment.

Continued Stay (Concurrent Review)

The UR performed the concurrent review on the next review date (hospital day 6) as indicated by the evidence-based clinical guidelines system; the guidelines were from the previous year and not updated to the current year, resulting in incorrect approved days of service.

Hospital Discharge and Care Transition to Home

The home health order was not specific to the services that would be provided to the member, the UR submits authorization for home health services to ensure the start of care within twenty-four hours, although services were delayed. Hospital discharge notification is sent to the assigned CM. CMS sends a letter of approval for home care by mail. The HP CM was not made aware of previous ER encounters and did not have access to pharmacy and PCP information. The completed care plan is sent to the CMS after ninety days.

Case Study

PRESENTATION

A seventy-five-year-old male enrolled in a Medicare/Medicaid plan presented to the primary care physician (PCP) office late Friday afternoon with chest pain, shortness of breath (SOB), fatigue, and history of coronary artery disease (CAD), hypertension, diabetes, gout, and increasing/ongoing complaints of leg cramps and muscle tenderness, which he believes is caused by cholesterol medication he discontinued taking six months ago. The member had three previous PCP visits over the past year regarding his complaints with no improvement.

EXAMINATION

The physical exam showed elevated BP (180/110), increased heart rate (HR) (130), sweating, and abnormal heart sounds. The PCP called EMS and had the member transported to the nearest hospital for emergency stabilization and management.

ER STABILIZATION TO HOSPITAL ADMISSION

The member arrived via ambulance from the PCP office with elevated blood pressure and heart rate and abnormal EKG. The member was placed on telemetry with three liters of oxygen (O_2), blood sugar (BS) of 400, and positive troponin levels. BP and HR remained unchanged, and the member was admitted with a diagnosis (Dx) of atherosclerotic heart disease with one blocked artery and unstable angina to progressive care unit (PCU) for cardiac monitoring and consultation. The hospital patient financial services called the after-hours number for the utilization management (UM) department of the HP to notify of the emergency admission and obtain an authorization number. The HP after hours was limited to discharge coordination of care only and did not handle any admission or authorization issues for new inpatient request; the HP was closed until Monday.

INITIAL REVIEW AND RETROSPECTIVE REVIEW OF WEEKEND

The UR contacted the hospital Monday afternoon (hospital day 3) after reviewing admission, discharge, transfer (ADT) data, which indicated member admission to a nonparticipating out-of-network (OON) hospital to request clinical documentation to evaluate the severity of the member's condition and the appropriateness of the treatment and services. The clinical information received summarized the following: "Patient remained stable with no further chest pain, SOB, BS range 88–120 without additional coverage, BP range 110/72 to 122/78 since admission. Telemonitor indicates normal sinus rhythm (NSR) since admission to the monitored floor, ambulating and planned for cardiac catheterization today." However, the member did not meet the clinical guidelines for acute inpatient but rather met the clinical guidelines for observation level of care only. The case was reviewed with the medical director and approved for inpatient admission and to continue with daily concurrent review until discharge.

Since the hospital is a nonparticipating OON provider, the UR implements the HP standard of practice and working process in emergent expedited OON request and completes single case agreements (SCAs). The UR discovered that the system did not accommodate automated data retrieval from OON providers or send payment.

CONTINUED STAY (CONCURRENT REVIEW)

The UR performed the concurrent review on the next review date (hospital day 6) as indicated by the evidence-based clinical guidelines system; the guidelines were from the previous year and not updated to the current year, resulting in incorrect approved days of service. Based on the clinical information received from the hospital, the cardiac catheterization showed blockages that require a cardiac procedure as urgent intervention, and the member was scheduled for one stent angioplasty today and would possibly go home tomorrow. The UR approved the concurrent review and updated the authorization accordingly. The UR scheduled the concurrent review (hospital day 7) for today yet receives a call that the member is being discharged now with order for home health.

HOSPITAL DISCHARGE AND CARE TRANSITION TO HOME

The UR receives the order for home health; even though the order was not specific as to the target focus of the services that would be provided to the member, the UR submits authorization for home health services to include RN evaluation for cardiac disease education with medication reconciliation and management and PT evaluation to the capitated home care provider to coordinate, facilitate, and ensure the start of care within twenty-four hours, although services were delayed by five days. In addition, the UR sends hospital discharge and care transition notification to the assigned HP CM as directed in the care transition standard of practice and working process. The information included a summary of the hospitalization and additional recommendation that the member would benefit from having a low-fat, low-sodium cardiac diet, meal prep/planning, and other community referrals. Once the home health agency and member were notified and confirmed by the fulfillment capitated vendor, the care management system sent confirmation of the start of care to the UR, PCP on record, and attending physician and sends a letter of approval for home care to the member by mail. The HP CM was not made aware of previous ER encounters and member participation in other HP programs and did not have access to pharmacy vendor and PCP information in the care management system. The HP CM completed the assessment and care plan and sent it to the CMS after ninety days.

Phases and Opportunities

Note: Opportunities and What's Not Happening are not applicable to some phases.

1. Member Seeks Treatment from Provider (PCP)

THE MEMBER JOURNEY

WHAT'S HAPPENING

The PCP gives treatment to members and has some collaboration with health plans and other providers.

WHAT'S NOT HAPPENING

Opportunity: Enhanced Integrated Co.—Management Care Management Coordination Model with PCP

Presentation

A seventy-five-year-old male enrolled in Medicare/Medicaid plan. Suffers from chest pain, shortness of breath (SOB), fatigue, history of coronary artery disease (CAD), hypertension, diabetes, gout, leg cramps, and muscle tenderness. He had three previous PCP visits over the past year regarding his complaints with no improvement."

*Reference the case study Presentation section to evaluate the members' ongoing challenges, PCP past treatment, and current action.

Innovation payment models offer diverse approaches to how we deliver care coordination and determine whether both the provider and the health plan were effective with their interaction and integration with the member in comanaging their needs, reducing hospitalization and readmissions, helping members improve their health, reducing the effects and incidence of chronic disease, and living healthier lives. In the scenario the member is dual-enrolled in Medicare and Medicaid. Medicaid is in the outpatient or community setting; therefore, member data was stratified to produce risk score, which determines the appropriateness of assignment to a CM and their level of engagement. The lack of evidence (the member had three previous PCP visits over the past year with complaints of leg cramps and muscle tenderness with no improvement) of this type of enhanced integration with the PCP and health plan resulted in missed opportunities to effectively integrate outpatient care delivery and management to address the member's physical and emotional concerns, provide education about his health condition and self-management tools that facilitate confidence, and promote resilience.

In addition, both health plans and providers are required to follow CMS Interoperability and Patient Access final rules and compliance to support effective integration. It requires state Medicaid agencies, Medicaid managed care plans, Children's Health Insurance Program (CHIP) agencies, and CHIP managed care entities to make certain health information about Medicaid and CHIP beneficiaries (members) is accessible through a Patient Access application program interface (API).

2. Provider Validates Member Insurance Benefits and Notifies Plan of Proposed Treatment

Provider validates member insurance benefits and notifies plan of proposed treatment.

2

THE MEMBER JOURNEY

WHAT'S HAPPENING

The PCP office validates insurance coverage/benefits by contacting the HP for prospective review (planned elective procedure).

*In the case study, this step is omitted due to the member experiencing chest pain, shortness of breath, and fatigue requiring emergency transfer to acute hospital for treatment and stabilization.

3. HP Receives Request for Authorization or Services from Member or Provider

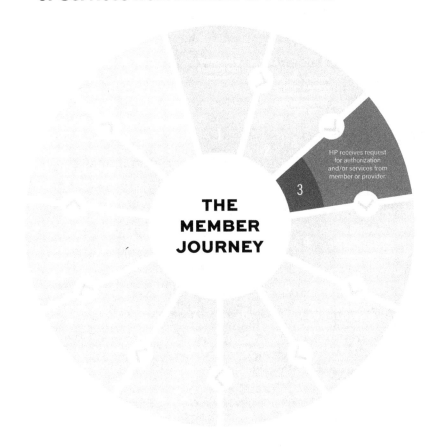

HP receives request for authorization and/or services from member or provider.

3

THE
MEMBER
JOURNEY

WHAT'S HAPPENING

The member arrived via ambulance from the PCP office with an elevated BP and HR and abnormal EKG. He was placed on telemetry with 3 l of O_2, BS of 400, and positive troponin. BP and HR remain unchanged. He was admitted with a Dx of atherosclerotic heart disease with one blocked artery and unstable angina to PCU for cardiac monitoring and consultation. The hospital (nonparticipating OON provider) patient financial services called the after-hours number for the UM department of the HP to notify of the emergency admission and obtain an authorization number. The HP after hours was limited to discharge coordination of care only and did not handle any admission or authorization issues for inpatient, as the health plan is closed until Monday.

WHAT'S NOT HAPPENING

Opportunity: Adoption of New Interoperability Methods for Exchanging Member Inpatient Notification Data and Process for Handling Nonparticipating Provider Request.

Initial Review and Retrospective Review of Weekend

Monday afternoon (hospital day 3). ADT indicated member admission to a nonparticipating out-of-network (OON) hospital and summarized the following: "Patient remained stable with no further chest pain, SOB, BS range 88–120, BP range 110/72 to 122/78, normal sinus rhythm (NSR), and planned for cardiac catheterization today." Did not meet guidelines for acute inpatient. Observation care only. The case was approved for inpatient admission and to continue with daily concurrent review until discharge. Care management system lacks the ability to automate data retrieval from OON providers or send payment.

*Reference the case study Initial Review and Retrospective Review of Weekend section

Deficient data exchange in healthcare has historically diminished member care, leading to poor health outcomes and higher costs. CMS Interoperability and the Patient Access final rule establishes policies that break down barriers in the nation's health system to enable better member access to their health information, improve interoperability, and unleash innovation while reducing the burden on HPs and providers. Members and their healthcare providers will have the opportunity to be more informed, which can lead to better care and improved member outcomes while reducing burden. In a future where data flows freely and securely between HPs, providers, and members, we can achieve truly coordinated care, improved health outcomes, and reduced costs. Some requirements include the following:

- Medicaid managed care plans and CHIP managed care entities to comply with a beneficiary's (member's) request to have their health data transferred from HP to HP, including encounter data, clinical information, and authorization status

- To exchange certain data with CMS daily on beneficiaries (members) who are dually eligible for Medicaid and Medicare for improved accuracy

- To design, develop, install, or enhance claims processing and information retrieval systems to meet regulatory expectations

The CMS also requires services to be provided within the HP provider network. If this option is not available, there are provisions for nonparticipating, out-of-network (OON) providers. If a member receives services, it must be reasonable and necessary for the Dx or treatment of an illness or injury and within the scope of a benefit category.

The Affordable Care Act (ACA) requires an HP to reimburse OON emergency services at least the greater of: (1) the amount the HP has negotiated with participating providers for emergency services (and if more than one amount is negotiated, the median of the amounts), (2) 100 percent of the allowed amount for services provided by a nonparticipating provider (i.e., the amount that the HP would pay in the absence of any cost sharing that would otherwise apply for services of nonparticipating OON providers), or (3) the amount that would be paid under Medicare.

It is best practice to create criteria for approving OON services, reviewing the criteria for appropriateness, and issuing approval authorization for services based on CMS guidelines below. There were missed opportunities in the case scenario where the health plan failed to evaluate the appropriateness for authorization of a nonparticipating facility to render the care and determine if the member condition was stable and appropriate for transferring to a participating facility, and their care management system lacks the ability to automate data retrieval from OON providers or send payment. The criteria for approving OON services are as follows:

1. OON Service Request (Facility and Provider). If all meets the criteria, the UR would approve the services request and complete the single case agreement (SCA):

    ➡ Services covered in the member's benefit plan and provider eligible to participate in government-funded programs

    ➡ Cannot be reasonably provided in network in a timely manner (timely = within thirty days of an acute, nonurgent condition)

    ➡ Referred by a participating/in-network provider or specialist to a higher-level facility due to complexity of the member condition that transfer or lengthy travel to an in-network provider would further exacerbate the condition

    ➡ Provider/facility willing to accept single case agreement for the care of member

2. Concurrent Review for Approved OON Hospital Care. The UR would incorporate the concurrent review that focuses on reviewing the patient's progress, prognosis, responsiveness to current treatment, and appropriate resource usage, adding this criterion: active course of treatment for an acute medical condition or an acute episode of a chronic condition that could be detrimental to the beneficiary if a change of provider occurred. Before facilitating OON care transition, UR are also encouraged to seek input from the beneficiary's (member) individualized care team when making utilization decisions. Additionally they must also consider the characteristics of the local delivery system available for specific members, to include

- availability of skilled nursing facilities, subacute care facilities, or home care in the service area to support the member after hospital discharge;

- availability of inpatient, outpatient, and transitional facilities;

- availability of outpatient services in lieu of inpatient services;

- availability of specialists in the area;

- availability of highly specialized services, such as transplant facilities or cancer centers;

- local hospitals' ability to provide all recommended services within the estimated length of stay; and

- submission to medical director for final decision.

3. Continuity of Care for Approved OON Outpatient Services.

    ➡ Beneficiary (member) has up to ninety days from the date of enrollment or until condition is resolved, whichever comes first, for follow-up care and treatment.

    ➡ Extensions beyond ninety days may be allowed if beneficiary (member) has relocated and awaits disenrollment.

Before making any continuity-of-care extensions, the UR should use UM criteria applied on a case-by-case basis to incorporate individual needs and to assess the local delivery system for applicable resources or alternatives and must consider at least the following factors when applying criteria to an individual:

1. Results of health risk assessment (HRA)

2. Beneficiary's individualized care plan

3. Age

4. Complications

5. Psychosocial situation

6. Home environment

7. Comorbidities

8. Progress of treatment

9. Access and availability of required services

10. Coverage of benefits

*Reference appendix for CMS federal statutes.

4. HP Reviews for Appropriateness and Notifies Provider and Member of Approved Determination

THE
MEMBER
JOURNEY

4   HP reviews for appropriateness and notifies provider and member of approved determination.

WHAT'S HAPPENING

The UR contacted the hospital Monday afternoon (hospital day 3) after reviewing ADT data, which indicated the member's admission to the nonparticipating OON hospital to request clinical documentation to evaluate the severity of the member's condition and the appropriateness of the treatment and services. The clinical information received summarized the following: "Patient remained stable with no further chest pain, SOB, BS range 88–120 without additional coverage, BP range 110/72 to 122/78 since admission. Telemonitor indicates normal sinus rhythm (NSR) since admission to the monitored floor, ambulating and planned for cardiac catheterization today."

WHAT'S NOT HAPPENING

Opportunity: New Interoperability Methods' Adoption for Prior Authorization Request.

ER Stabilization to Hospital Admission

Arrived via ambulance with elevated blood pressure and heart rate and abnormal EKG. Placed on telemetry with three liters of oxygen (O2), blood sugar (BS) of 400, and positive troponin levels. Admitted with a diagnosis (Dx) of atherosclerotic heart disease with one blocked artery and unstable angina to progressive care unit (PCU). Financial services called the after-hours number for the UM department to obtain authorization number. HP after-hours was limited to discharge coordination of care only; the HP was closed until Monday.

Initial Review and Retrospective Review of Weekend

Monday afternoon (hospital day 3). ADT indicated member admission to a nonparticipating out-of-network (OON) hospital and summarized the following: "Patient remained stable with no further chest pain, SOB, BS range 88–120, BP range 110/72 to 122/78, normal sinus rhythm (NSR), and planned for cardiac catheterization today." Did not meet guidelines for acute inpatient. Observation care only. The case was approved for inpatient admission and to continue with daily concurrent review until discharge. Care management system lacks the ability to automate data retrieval from OON providers or send payment.

*Reference the case study ER Stabilization to Hospital Admission and Initial Review and Retrospective Review of Weekend sections.

HPs that are contracted with the CMS use an integrated approach to ensure access to covered services consistent with requirements and to coordinate and promote optimal utilization of healthcare resources; make utilization decisions that affect the healthcare of beneficiaries (members) in a fair, impartial, and consistent manner; and assist with transition to alternative care when benefits end, should an enrollee be no longer eligible for benefits, continuing to build on its road map to improve interoperability and health information access for members, providers, and HPs.

When implemented effectively, health information exchange (interoperability) can also reduce the burden of certain administrative processes, such as prior authorization. Some HPs have leveraged these new technologies to enhance communication between providers and facilities that ensures timely services to members and reduces the administrative burden in an efficient manner. This is a new era of quality and lower costs in healthcare, as HPs and providers will now have access to complete member histories through accessing patient information (API), reducing unnecessary care and allowing for more coordinated and seamless member care.

Hospitals and providers can currently submit an authorization request through various methods 24 hours, 7 days a week, 365 days per year such as

- HP self-service portal and submission of authorization templates and

- Electronic Data Interchange (EDI) 278 directly to the HP EDI submission or through a clearinghouse.

The regulations will drive change in how clinical and administrative information is exchanged between HPs, providers, and members and will support standardized clinical documentation submissions across HPs and more efficient care coordination. These new policies may reduce burdens of the prior authorization process by increasing automation and encouraging improvements in policies and procedures to streamline decision-making and communications. In the case scenario, the HP failed to have after hours and weekend UM department hours available to process the expedited request within the twenty-four-hour timeframe, and there were limited methods for providers seeking authorization to treat members in a timely manner.

5. HP Tracks Utilization and Quality of All Services at All Levels of Care (e.g., Inpatient, Outpatient Services) through Discharge and Ensures Timely Care Transition Notification

THE
MEMBER
JOURNEY

5

HP tracks utilization and quality of all services at all levels of care (e.g., inpatient, outpatient services) through discharge and ensures timely care transition notification.

WHAT'S HAPPENING

The concurrent review focuses on the member's progress, prognosis, response to current treatment, and appropriate resource usage while facilitating successful care transitions.

The UR performed the concurrent review on the next review date (hospital day 6) as indicated by the evidence-based clinical guidelines system. Based on the clinical information received from the hospital, the cardiac catheterization showed blockages that require a cardiac procedure as an urgent intervention, and the member was scheduled for one stent angioplasty today and would possibly go home tomorrow. The UR approved the concurrent review and updated the authorization accordingly. The UR has scheduled a concurrent review (hospital day 7) for today yet receives a call that the member is being discharged now with order for home health.

WHAT'S NOT HAPPENING

Opportunity: Enhanced Care Management System to Include Cloud Evidence-Based Clinical Guidelines.

Continued Stay (Concurrent Review)

The UR performed the concurrent review on the next review date (hospital day 6) as indicated by the evidence-based clinical guidelines system; the guidelines were from the previous year and not updated to the current year, resulting in incorrect approved days of service.

*Reference the case study Continued Stay (Concurrent Review) section.

The UR performed a concurrent review the next review date (hospital day 6) as indicated by the evidence-based clinical guidelines system, but the guidelines were from the previous year and not updated to the current year. The member was inappropriately approved for two days instead of one day in misalignment to the latest clinical guidelines application, accessible through popular web browsers with automatic updates, and reduced maintenance requirements.

6. Utilization Reviewer (Nurse or Pharmacy Technician with Support of Physician If Required) Sends Care Transition Notification and Referrals to HP CM

THE MEMBER JOURNEY

6

Utilization Reviewer (UR), (nurse or pharmacy technician with support of physician if required) sends care transition notification and referrals to HP Care Manager (CM).

WHAT'S HAPPENING

The UR confirms member discharge from the acute level of care, PCU, in which the member was admitted, and the member discharge disposition. The UR sent notification of discharge to the HP CM, initiating care transition workflow. The notification referral should include the following:

- Admitting Dx, procedures, and dates of services (admission to discharge)

- Facility and attending physician's name

- Summary of hospitalization (hospital discharge summary, discharge instruction with medication if available)

- Outpatient discharge orders and finalized authorizations with provider names

- Additional referral recommendations based on member gaps

- Member data (history of previous ER/urgent care, inpatient encounters with clinical documentation)

- PCP/pharmacy data

- Previous activity in HP and external CM programs

The UR sent hospital discharge and care transition notification to the assigned HP CM as directed in the care transition standard of practice and working process. The information included the summary of the hospitalization, additional recommendation that the member would benefit from having a low-fat, low-sodium cardiac diet and meal prep/planning, and other community referrals.

WHAT'S NOT HAPPENING

Opportunity: Improved UR and HP CM Communication and Enhanced Care Management System Integration.

Hospital Discharge and Care Transition to Home

The home health order was not specific to the services that would be provided to the member, the UR submits authorization for home health services to ensure the start of care within twenty-four hours, although services were delayed. Hospital discharge notification is sent to the assigned CM. CMS sends a letter of approval for home care by mail. The HP CM was not made aware of previous ER encounters and did not have access to pharmacy and PCP information. The completed care plan is sent to the CMS after ninety days.

*Reference the case study Hospital Discharge and Care Transition to Home section.

The HP CM was not made aware of previous ER encounters and member participation in other HP programs and did not have access to pharmacy vendor and PCP information in the care management system.

It is more effective to include a verbal phone call from the UR to the HP CM in addition to sending a notification during member handoff to discuss all relevant information to guide the member care plan, including previous ER encounters/claims and member participation in other internal and external care management programs with outcomes.

In addition, the HP CM will benefit from system optimization aligned with the CMS Interoperability and Patient Access final rule, including a bidirectional data feed from provider/external vendors to the HP with access provided to appropriate care management team members.

7. HP CM Receives Discharge Notification and Discharging Facility Documentation to Begin the Appropriate Care Transitions

THE
MEMBER
JOURNEY

7

HP CM receives
discharge
notification and
discharging
facility docu-
mentation to
begin the
appropriate care
transitions.

8. **HP CM Coordinates with Entire Healthcare Team, Including, but Not Limited to, PCP, Specialists, Hospital, Skilled Nursing Facility (SNF), Rehabilitation, Long-Term Acute Care, Nursing Home, Medical Supply Vendor, and Community Organizations**

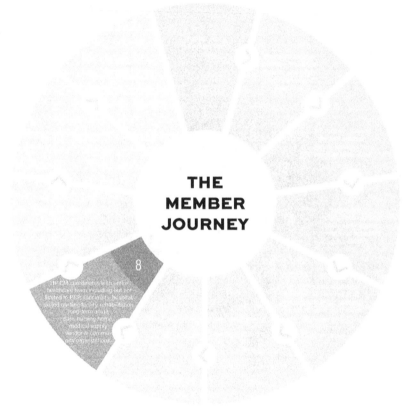

THE
MEMBER
JOURNEY

WHAT'S HAPPENING

This is a very perilous step; care coordination brings all internal and external healthcare team members together, including PCP, specialists, hospital, community clinics/organizations, rehabilitation facility, behavioral health inpatient/outpatient facility, home health agencies, palliative care, hospice inpatient/outpatient facility, pharmacy, and medical supply vendors, to discuss member health and social needs, self-care challenges, and discharge instructions and align with a plan of care. Based on the scenario, the HP CM coordinated with the PCP, home health agency, and outpatient community services to ensure treatment plans are included in member HP (condition care program) care plan. The HP CM also confirmed the start of home health services and connected with the CMS to validate Medicaid/Medicare community resources and programs available to the member—for example, long-term services and support (LTSS), including Program of All-Inclusive Care for the Elderly (PACE) and special needs plan (SNP).

WHAT'S NOT HAPPENING

Opportunity: Improved Communication with Care Transitions to Outpatient Services and Risk Reporting to CMS.

Hospital Discharge and Care Transition to Home

The home health order was not specific to the services that would be provided to the member, the UR submits authorization for home health services to ensure the start of care within twenty-four hours, although services were delayed. Hospital discharge notification is sent to the assigned CM. CMS sends a letter of approval for home care by mail. The HP CM was not made aware of previous ER encounters and did not have access to pharmacy and PCP information. The completed care plan is sent to the CMS after ninety days.

*Reference the case study Hospital Discharge and Care Transition to Home section.

In the scenario home health visits were delayed and did not start until five days after the member was discharged. It's imperative for HPs to monitor and take action, as necessary, to improve continuity and coordination of care across the healthcare network to prevent harm to members, including

- tracking movement of the member between intermittent and ongoing healthcare practitioners and across inpatient/outpatient settings as their conditions and care needs change during a chronic or acute illness,

- collecting data to evaluate and document the progress of transitions,

- reaching out to healthcare practitioners and facilitating to resolve risks, and

- reporting issues unresolvable with providers to the CMS.

The HP CM will benefit from communicating with the home health agency immediately after the member was discharged to ensure visits start within twenty-four hours. If the home health agency is unable to meet the time frame, the HP CM should work with the member to find another home health agency and report the original agency to the CMS.

9. HP CM Performs Assessment and Develops Member Care Plan

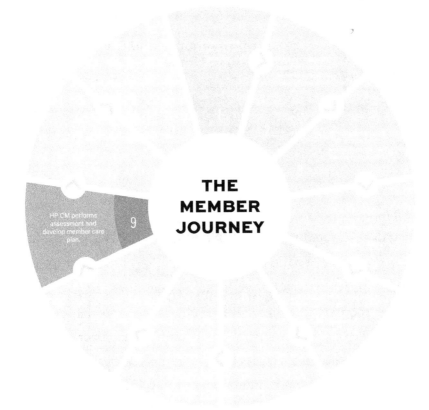

WHAT'S HAPPENING

The HP CM has some knowledge of the member's habits, medical history, and treatment plan from providers, so information is added to the care plan and completed after member assessment. Initial assessments are due within ninety days per CMS guidelines.

WHAT'S NOT HAPPENING

Opportunity: Care Management System Enhancement to Include Alert and Hard Stop Features.

Hospital Discharge and Care Transition to Home

The home health order was not specific to the services that would be provided to the member, the UR submits authorization for home health services to ensure the start of care within twenty-four hours, although services were delayed. Hospital discharge notification is sent to the assigned CM. CMS sends a letter of approval for home care by mail. The HP CM was not made aware of previous ER encounters and did not have access to pharmacy and PCP information. The completed care plan is sent to the CMS after ninety days.

*Reference the case study Hospital Discharge and Care Transition to Home section.

Based on the scenario, the HP CM was aware that the member was recently discharged from the hospital and prioritized outreach. During the assessment call with the member, the HP CM asked member-specific questions to understand how he is managing his CAD, diabetes, and gout. After completion the member responses triggered auto-generated goals to help him move to healthier lifestyle changes for overall health improvement to decrease medical utilization. The HP CM scheduled the member for a follow-up call within health plan time frame protocol to initiate goal work and actionable interventions. The HP CM also completed required documentation but submitted the assessment to the CMS after ninety days.

To avoid missing timely submissions, HPs can safeguard care management systems with alert and hard stop features to prevent member case exit without assessment and care plan submission within specified time frames.

10. HP CM Manages Member Care Plan Goals and Interventions

HP CM manage member care plan goals and interventions.

10

THE MEMBER JOURNEY

WHAT'S HAPPENING

Prior to calling the member, the HP CM reviewed previous notes, populated goals, and external programs available to the member, offered through the CMS (LTSS, PACE, SNP). During the call the HP CM assessed if the member was having current medical condition symptoms, confirmed home health visits started, and cardiac rehabilitation was scheduled, then moved on to prioritized goals work, including the following:

- Healthy heart diet – based on member habit of eating fried foods four times a week, contributing to his elevated cholesterol levels, blocked heart vessel, and recent surgery

- Understanding of cholesterol test – based on member's lack of understanding of his cholesterol lab results during assessment response

- Medication compliance – based on member's missing cholesterol medication, Lipitor, most days of the week during member assessment response and pharmacy and hospital history and physical examination (H&P) notes.

The HP CM taught the member about foods included in a healthy heart diet and offered a referral to an HP internal dietitian for weekly meal planning, whom the member agreed to call. The HP CM also educated the member on the importance of taking his Lipitor daily and risks if missed; the member agreed to educational mailing and a referral to an internal HP pharmacist. While doing a pulse check on call duration, the HP CM noticed that the member was distracted and less interested and so offered cholesterol test education for the next call.

Lastly, the HP CM identified the member as a high-risk elderly adult who lives alone and is adamant about maintaining his independence and so offered information about CMS LTSS programs that support older adults who want to stay home with access to community services like Meals on Wheels, transportation to doctor appointments/pharmacy, and home visits from doctors, social worker, and dietitian. The member agreed for the HP CM to initiate coordination with the CMS and discuss further on the next call. After the call ended, the HP CM completed documentation and submitted referrals to internal health professionals and the CMS.

11. HP CM Provides Ongoing Member Support and Follow-Up

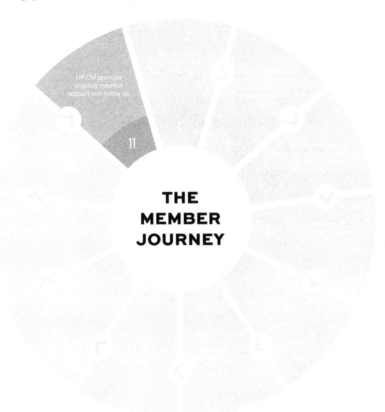

THE
MEMBER
JOURNEY

WHAT'S HAPPENING

The HP CM will reassess the member for any new challenges related to his medical conditions, continue working on goals until the progression target is met or the member requests to stop, and collaborate with all internal and external care team members, including HP health professionals, home health, CMS CM, and cardiac rehabilitation to ensure services were completed, the member is progressing as expected, and there are no quality concerns.

Technology Considerations

An effective care management system with interoperability, integration, interface, automation, baseline, and customized rule engines to meet compliance requirements is critical to support operational delivery. The system must include bidirectional integration to pull medical and pharmacy encounter activity and claims into UM/CM platforms, retrieve and send out ADT data, and transmit provider data (test, procedure, clinical information, progress notes) from their external systems into the member assessment and care plan. Internal UM/CM team members must be able to view all care management platforms with associated business units (UM, CM, appeals, enrollment, etc.) for a 360 view of the member. The care management system should also have fax and mail fulfillment vendor integration and built-in benefits and accumulators. Unfortunately, lack of system integration is another industry trend impacting member services. Most health plans only meet a few of these requirements and face productivity, quality, and compliance challenges.

Understanding system capabilities and partnering with health information management (HIM)/IT teams to improve and manage capabilities enhances your industry expertise. You will have the ability to quickly identify gaps and resolve without experiencing financial, quality, or growth loss.

Here is a handy yet *impactful checklist* you can use to reevaluate your current care management system or when considering a new one. Many times, these items are considered enhancements and often not explored, resulting in organization-wide, permanent work-arounds exhausting more resources to complete tasks not reported in the system. Therefore, it is imperative to take time to collectively work in tandem to ensure the system vendors understand your requirements and current work-arounds. Enabled technology advancements must be integrated to be actionable with the incorporation of all vendor partners' data and the entire spectrum of care and service. It is no longer considered an "enhancement"; it is now called a "must-have" and is required.

CARE MANAGE-MENT SYSTEM FEATURES	DESCRIPTION
Real-Time, Comprehensive, Member-Centric Data; Quality Measures; and Line of Business (LOB) Compliance Integration within the Dashboard and Member/Provider Portal	A 360 view of the member displays a quick view of real-time member engagement updates, including all forms of contact in care services. Features include: • social determinants of health (SDoH) integration with vendor partners, associated community referrals, and appropriate documentation; • SDoH stratification with real-time alerts that streamlines HP CM assignment for target and focus engagement; • NCQA HEDIS, population health, and contract compliance for specific LOB, including state/federal contract requirements and ad hoc reporting; • integration of PCP/specialist office and hospital data, notes, and records, including ancillary providers (e.g., home health), arrival/departure times, videos, etc. • organization-wide level document and correspondence, ability to secure specific documents based on user or groups; • ability to manually add nonparticipating or OON providers to the care management system based on their national provider identifier (NPI) to ensure efficiency and continuation of care; • automated quality compliance scan to capture and close care gaps from integrated information retrieval; • dispensing pharmacy location, medication and ordering physician data, refill pickup, and special programs such as substance abuse and opiates lock-ins

Automation and Real-Time Interoperability Authorizations, Referrals, Service Request, and Comprehensive Utilization Management Functions/Features	• Automate decision-driven requests such as prior authorization based on integration member clinical data information, including psychosocial determinants of health, measures of health/health status, and documentation of care delivery • Enable providers to send prior authorization requests (and receive responses electronically) directly from the provider's electronic health record (EHR) or other practice management system • Auto-review criteria rule and authorization processing via Health Level (HL)7/Fast Health Interoperability Resources (FHIR) • Auto-create and auto-determine authorization request and criteria rules from fax or authorization template • Send appropriate correspondence and capture date/time when received and determined • Auto-route via rules engine to next UR, adhering to time frames and case status, and send automated notification of care transitions and referrals to ancillary providers in preparation for discharge
Automation and Interoperability Comprehensive Care and Behavioral Management Functions/Features	• Automate notification of care transition to HP CM, PCP, member, and responsible party upon discharge from higher level of care and return to baseline level of care based on ADT/integrated hospital/subacute/SNF data • Send correspondence notification to member and provider portal, schedule appointment with options for telehealth within five days and no longer than seven days postdischarge • Have the ability to capture date/time of verbal, written, and fax notifications • Auto-enroll in care transition care management program • Auto-schedule HP CM assessment and care plan meeting within fourteen days from discharge • Stratify new enrollee/population for HP CM engagement based on employer group/state/federal contract and assign according to policy of caseload • Have NCQA-approved assessment preloaded for all populations to include general, maternity, infants, NICU, teens, young adults, older adults/seniors, mental health and illness, and disease and health-specific condition • NCQA-approved care plans that are generated from the approved assessments

Quality of Care, Member/Provider Appeals and Grievances	• Have access and role-based security • Meet CMS federal requirements for appeals, grievances, and organization determination documentation and time frames for Medicaid or Medicare health plans
Single Sign-On (SSO), Real-Time Web Services w/ Mobility, API Integration	• Single sign-on with all plan applications • Real-time integration with all Wi-Fi/wearable technology in the care management system, member, and provider portal with actionable triggers for intervention • iPad integration/electronic signature and archive telehealth sessions • Health fairs and biometrics integration • Decisions support criteria integration

Project Requirements for System Implementation

According to the Project Management Institute (PMI), 71 percent of projects either fail outright or are "challenged"—projects deliver fewer features and functions than the customer expects, are completed overbudget, or are completed behind schedule. I supported several care management system implementation projects, realizing the most important element was flawed, gathering accurate requirements.

So how do HPs and vendors ensure accurate requirements gathering and documenting? At the basic level, every project has two types of requirements: business requirements (what) and technical requirements (how). Business requirements define what the organization wants or needs to be able to do once the project is completed. They describe the changes in capabilities that will result from the project. Technical requirements define solutions for how each project need will be satisfied. These solutions are directly linked to one or more business requirements.

As project stakeholders define the business needs for their project, it is necessary to look beyond the obvious functional requirements covering the core business capabilities associated with business processes. Stakeholders should also consider interface requirements, which are capabilities driven by the external entities. Additionally nonfunctional or supporting requirements can be uncovered by ensuring that meetings include participation beyond core business stakeholders. Nonfunctional requirements vary by type of project and industry but typically include

- audit requirements,

- security requirements,

- information movement requirements,

- reporting requirements, and

- information integrity (validation/edit) requirements.

Business Requirement Facilitated Meetings

Several meetings should be held, especially with agile projects, executing multiple deliverables in three- to four-week sprints. HPs should expect the project manager to initially arrange several (two to three) collaborative meetings a day, focused on defining business requirements. The first business requirement meeting focuses on the higher level or "parent" requirements. Parent-level requirements include conceptual needs across all business processes, interfaces, and support requirement categories. The secondary business requirement meetings drill down these parent requirements into detailed business requirements or "child" requirements.

In the beginning business requirements are brainstormed without regard to which business process they fall under. After the brainstorm the requirements are clarified and categorized under one of the business processes. If stakeholders find they are unable to categorize the business requirement under just one business process, this means they have a gap that needs to be resolved. Causes of this gap include the following:

- The business requirement is not specific enough and may need to be broken into multiple statements, with each statement describing a need specific to the functionality associated with a business process.

- The business requirement is out of scope for the project, which is why it does not have a business process it fits under.

- The business requirement is valid, but the team discovers that there is a missing business process that should have been included as part of the project scope. After securing approval to add the business process, additional brainstorming is needed to identify other missing requirements that belong to the new business process.

During business requirement meetings, the mix of business and technical project stakeholders consists of 90 percent business stakeholders and 10 percent technical stakeholders. Although most organizations prefer to bring the technical team in meetings later, a small technical team should be a part of early meetings to provide insight as to whether a business requirement is clear enough for the technical team to use when considering solution options later in the project. They can also help identify when a requirement is too vague or appears to contain a solution. The focus of the business requirement meetings is to ensure that stakeholders agree on business requirements that state the needed business capabilities without describing how to find solutions for the need.

Requirements Definition: Documenting the How for a Project

Once the project team is aligned with the business requirements, which clearly state the needs for the project, they expand the requirement statements to include solutions. By using the business requirement statements as the driver for documenting the project's how and tying each solution directly to the business need, the team ensures that the project includes only solutions that are in scope for the project. This minimizes the risk of using the project as a mechanism to justify a solution rather than to address a defined business need. By using this technique, solutions can be traced all the way back to the business processes that were expected to change and to the objectives that the organization expected to meet.

Technical Requirement Facilitated Meetings

Project stakeholders should use collaborative facilitated meetings, scheduled over two- to three-day periods, to define the technical requirements. During technical requirement facilitated meetings, the mix of project stakeholders flips to 90 percent technical stakeholders and 10 percent business stakeholders. Again, it is highly recommended to include both types of stakeholders in these meetings. Business stakeholders provide value by confirming that the business need has not been missed or changed in an attempt to drive to a solution. They also confirm, early on in the project, that if the proposed solution is developed, it will, in fact, address the real business need and not create a negative impact on business processes.

Sometimes multiple technical approaches can exist for the project solution. When this situation occurs, it is best for project stakeholders to assess each approach individually, comparing them side by side and identifying the pros and cons, in an attempt to select one approach for defining the technical requirements. If one technical approach cannot be determined as the most viable approach, the meeting facilitator will ensure that stakeholders are aligned with the multiple approaches being considered. The meeting discussion will need to document detailed technical requirement statements for each technical approach being considered. As the details of each solution are clarified, it generally becomes easier for the project team to make a clear decision on one approach over another or possibly to discover a new or blended approach to meet the project's needs.

Ensuring Requirement Traceability throughout the Project Life Cycle

By defining the boundaries of the project effort at the beginning using the scope statement, project stakeholders will have established the framework for making all future project decisions and tracing the evolution of project requirement statements from high-level business needs (the what) to lower-level solutions (the how). HPs need to ensure they provide qualified representatives from all affected areas to minimize the risk of overlooking critical project needs. As business requirements are defined across business processes, consideration for functional requirements, interface requirements, and supporting non-functional capabilities needs to be included. To ensure that business requirements are both clear and in scope for the project, they must be mapped back to one business process defined during the project scoping activity.

Compliance

Lastly, it is critical for industry experts to understand regulatory agencies' standards/mandates to meet compliance. Missing this step will significantly impact operational delivery, resulting in penalties/ sanctions and possible suspension or inability of the HP to market plans across exchange, commercial, Medicare, and Medicaid lines of business. Facing challenges with compliance requirements is also an industry trend negatively affecting several HPs across our nation. To avoid this, follow CMS, NCQA, and URAC accreditation and quality standards, which include a combination of documented processes, reports, materials, records, files, and model of care. Reference appendix page for more details.

Note: It is recommended to find an industry expert to review all regulatory accreditation and quality technical specification for more details; modifications are made annually. The information provided is up to date for the current year; check for changes in future years and make modifications to policies as needed.

As part of process improvement and ongoing evaluation, the care management industry incorporated population health and social determinants of health (SDoH) to assess critical factors affecting members' ability to move to healthy lifestyles and effectively manage specific populations using analytics and streamlined metrics. Reference appendix for more details.

BENEFITS OF BECOMING AN INDUSTRY EXPERT

- Being considered a trusted advisor from peers, subordinates, family, and friends

- Ability to develop a high-performing team and move to a center of excellence

- Ability to avoid regulatory penalties/sanctions, resulting in increased profitability

- Ability to identify operational gaps quickly and develop effective strategies

CONSEQUENCES OF NOT FURTHERING SELF-GROWTH

- Inability of your team to optimize operations and improve quality

- Loss of revenue related to sanctions/penalties

- Team not trusting your leadership, resulting in frustration and confusion

- High stress levels from operational risks and issues

BEGIN BY

- Learning regulatory agencies' (NCQA, URAC, CMS) compliance standards/mandates by participating in trainings and collaborating with compliance leaders and other healthcare experts

- Keeping up with yearly compliance standard/mandate updates

- Reviewing and understanding state/federal contracts with your organization

- Joining professional organizations within your company and externally (e.g., building a five-star Medicare organization, HEDIS discussion forum, and managed care executives on LinkedIn) and the Association of Health Insurance Plan (AHIP) and subscribing to regulatory agency and professional organization newsletters

- Participating in yearly seminars and conferences, for example, Medicare STARS, HEDIS, URAC quality and risk sessions, and AHIP Institute and Expo

- Referencing relevant white papers, journals, articles, podcasts, and blogs

Becoming an industry expert starts the moment you take account-ability and provide quality services whether or not a physical supervisor is in place. It happens in frontline positions and expands as you move to a leadership title. Remember, your goal as an industry expert is to be a resource for accurate information and follow guiding principles and leading practice methodologies, resulting in high-quality opera-tions and compliance and transforming your organization to a center of excellence. As a self-aware industry expert, you are now prepared to establish relationships with your team members by understanding who they are personally and professionally prior to enforcing rules.

CHAPTER 3

Establish Relationships with Your Team

Employees who believe that management is concerned about them as a whole person, not just an employee, are more productive, more satisfied, more fulfilled. Satisfied employees mean satisfied customers, which leads to profitability.

—ANNE MULCAHY

Throughout many years working with various companies and clients, I recognized a common element—leaders were predominately focused on the bottom line, which meant productivity ruled the day. It was common practice to ensure that staff started work on time, aligned with operational changes, and met performance metrics. Leaders heavily scrutinized subordinates' work, aiming for the pot of gold that would bring higher revenue and company growth. It was also a way of showing their personal achievement and earning another badge of honor to embellish their performance and dedication to the organization. Although this is an important aspect of leadership, I realized a fundamental principle was frequently missed—spending time with every team member, getting to know them before instructing them how to follow policies and procedures and dishing out corrective action if they didn't comply.

I remember leading a large team of advanced clinicians during a very complex project. I was brought on to improve processes, establish structure, and rebuild our credibility with a client. After gathering some information from my leaders regarding the current state of the project and the team, I decided to do a two-week assessment, including one-to-one meetings with all team members, to get to know them and their personal goals outside of work and at work. I asked questions like "Why did you choose this field, and what is your immediate need?" Prior to asking these questions, I assured them our discussions were confidential and would not be communicated to executive leaders based on individual responses but rather as group themes with a focus to improve opportunity trends.

It was eye opening to discover that most of them never had one-to-one meetings in the past, nor did they have the opportunity to voice their concerns, and more importantly they felt executive leaders didn't even know who they were. Many of them felt disconnected and unheard and harbored plans to leave the organization. I spent a significant amount of time talking to them about their families, their goals for the next few years, what they would like to see changed, and how I could best serve them. I also laid out some preliminary plans to improve work distribution, travel schedule, training, procedures, and communication from leaders and develop recognition campaigns with their participation. What impacted them most was feeling like someone finally cared enough to ask about their family, health, and ideas and simply being heard. In the end several of the team members did not resign as planned, instead looking forward to building a closer relationship with leaders and future operational plans.

The crux of that example is that the essence of nursing is compassion and caring, and this isn't something you can fake. Remember, when you don't respect the human side of things, it is a problem. The epigraph introducing this chapter is powerful; you can't simply hammer employees about productivity all the time. If you haven't gotten to know them and make them feel like they exist, they won't be productive in the first place.

We must bring the *human* back into human relations and think of our team like another family.

I always believe team members are any organization's most important asset. Their unique skills, personalities, and contributions are the foundation to an organization's culture and productivity and ultimately drive the bottom line. Without team members there is no business. We must bring the *human* back into human relations and think of our team like another family. As a leader you will be amazed to experience increased engagement, role satisfaction, and commitment that will seamlessly improve productivity!

What It Means to Establish Relationships with Your Team

Teams are like an extended family. When we think of family, imagine a group of people sharing a bond; and each person has a role to play that is entangled with communication, respect, trust, love, and loyalty. While a traditional family is led by parents, your team is led by leaders, but one family member is no more important than the other. They are strongest as a unit; when something happens to one, it happens to all, and everyone is impacted. Families strive to protect each other as they go into the world, facing new experiences.

In your role as a leader, it is wise to establish protection for your team first. Let them know you are not only supporting and driving their performance but also dedicated to build a safe bond with them, fostered by trust and respect. Always let them know you have their best interests at your core. In the beginning, schedule one-to-one meetings with each team member, accommodating their availability. Inform them you are setting some time aside to touch base with them to see how things are going. Emphasize it's not a meeting to evaluate their performance but more of an informal meeting to discuss their ideas. This messaging will decrease the anxiety of your team members, preventing them from wondering if they did something wrong, did not meet their performance targets, or are being terminated. To that end many of them will arrive to the meeting relaxed and eager to share information.

To help you prepare for these meetings, draft standardized questions and have some ideas how the team may respond. Jot down some guided responses to ensure you are delivering consistent information with everyone, understanding that some comments will be unique and require your best judgment and experience in the absence of prompting.

Recommended personal questions include the following:

1. **Tell me about yourself.** Allow them to introduce who they believe they are personally and professionally. As they tell their story, encourage them to recollect statements about family/friends (children, siblings, parents, grandparents, spouse, etc.). Usually someone from their family or close friend circle motivates them, and they aim to please them in various ways, like obtaining a college degree or GED, becoming a particular type of professional, earning a certain amount of money, or making a positive difference in our

world. This is a loaded question, so be patient and let them answer in its entirety—you may need to probe a little on specific responses to learn more or get clarity. This question sets the stage for building immediate trust because they have shared some precious things about themselves and will feel gratitude by you taking interest and listening. Make sure you tell your brief personal/career story as well.

2. **What are your personal goals for the next few months?** This is important to realize. Many leaders focus on long-term goals associated to their organization, but it's best to meet team members where they are; they may not be able to determine or commit to long-term goals or figure out if their current role is suitable for their needs at the moment based on what's going on in their life. You may hear responses like these:

   → "I'm hoping to move in a new apartment next month."

   → "I am trying to find permanent childcare for my kid."

   → "I am overwhelmed with taking care of my aging parents. No one else is helping me."

   → "I'm struggling with paying my bills."

   → "I'm trying to earn money to go back to school."

Your responses are critical, and understanding the immediate things your team members are striving for in their personal lives allows you to educate and get them connected to internal and external resources. Most importantly it shows you care.

3. **What are your expectations of me?** Although this will overlap with work-related questions, it is good to hear

comments aligned with how they envision a leader caring for them and supporting them as a whole person. Now you are ready to ask high-level work questions without mentioning performance measures or goals. Remember that this meeting is focused on rapport building. We will discuss other operational/performance meetings in the next chapter.

Recommended work questions include the following:

1. **How do you feel about the support you are receiving from your leaders and peers?** Use caution with this question. Team members may be intimidated by your role and uncomfortable with transparency. Prior to asking them this question, let them know you understand everyone has opportunities for growth, including you as a leader. Feel comfortable voicing your concerns; without complete disclosure, improvements will be limited. Relationship disconnect or distance is usually identified with responses.

2. **How was your training? Do you feel like you have what you need to do your job?** You will learn a lot with this question. Training deficits are an industry trend related to ineffective new-hire orientation and refresher courses, noninclusion of compliance standards in training, role confusion, complicated procedures/workflows that aren't working, and training tools missing key content.

3. **What is working well for you in your role?** This gives you the opportunity to measure your team members' happiness meter. Hopefully there are more things working well than not, but either way reassure them you are there to ensure their needs are met and that you will continue discussions.

4. **What is not working well?** Again, your team members may be hesitant to answer, but make it a point to build their confidence. You need the truth so you can begin tackling the most challenging gaps causing your team's frustrations, patient safety issues, compliance penalties, and loss of revenue and growth.

5. **If you had a magic wand, what would change immediately?** Allow your team the freedom and comfort to offer suggestions for improvement or voice concerns.

Remember that your team members are the boots on the ground. They are reviewing authorization requests, teaching members, documenting care plans, toggling through care management systems, and collaborating with providers, vendors, and community organizations every day. Through trial and error, they have discovered better ways to deliver services based on unfavorable experiences. Consider their feedback carefully; it just may work.

After the meetings thank your team for participating and advise them you will schedule routine informal and formal meetings in the near future, but feel free to ask questions and note you have an open-door policy.

The next critical step is to understand the various work styles of your team, how they comprehend knowledge, communicate, problem-solve, and execute work. We discussed at length in chapter 1, "Self-Awareness," the importance of discovering your work style as a leader and how you can best contribute to your organization. The same is required for your teams. Organizations that apply a methodical approach using leading practice principles are more successful in establishing healthy relationships with their team, providing customized role and responsibility guidance.

Require all team members to take an industry standard personality test like the Myers-Briggs indicator to determine their strengths and gifts to give to others and coach them how to apply recommendations.

Review of Personality Types

The Four Myers-Brigg© Preference Pairs

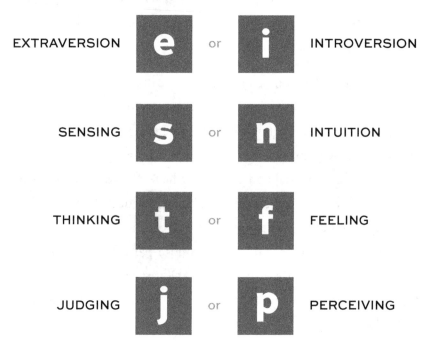

EXTRAVERSION	e	or	i	INTROVERSION
SENSING	s	or	n	INTUITION
THINKING	t	or	f	FEELING
JUDGING	j	or	p	PERCEIVING

Myers-Briggs personality types represent individuals' natural preferences in the four aspects of personality described, which account for the natural differences between people. People tend to develop behaviors, skills, and attitudes associated with their type, and individuals with types different from yours will likely be opposite to you in many ways.

There is no right or wrong to these preferences. Each identifies normal and valuable human behaviors, and each type has its own potential strengths as well as likely blind spots. Based on their answers, each of your team members will have four identified types from the list of eight personality types above (e.g., ENTP, ESTJ).

CHARACTERISTICS OF PERSONALITY TYPES

EXTROVERSION	INTROVERSION
• Drawn to the outside world • Prefer to communicate by talking • Work out ideas by talking them through • Learn best through doing or discussing • Have broad interests • Tend to be sociable and expressive • Readily take initiative in work and relationships	• Drawn to their inner world • Prefer to communicate in writing • Work out ideas by reflecting on them • Learn best by reflection, mental "practice" • Focus in depth on a few interests • Tend to be private and contained • Take initiative selectively—when the situation or issue is very important to them
SENSING	**INTUITION**
• Oriented to present realities • Factual and concrete • Focus on what is real and actual • Observe and remember specifics • Build carefully and thoroughly toward conclusions • Understand ideas and theories through practical applications • Trust experience	• Oriented to future possibilities • Imaginative and verbally creative • Focus on the patterns and meanings in data • Remember specifics when they relate to a pattern • Move quickly to conclusions; follow hunches • Want to clarify ideas and theories before putting them into practice • Trust inspiration

THINKING	FEELING
• Analytical • Use cause-and-effect reasoning • Solve problems with logic • Strive for an objective standard of truth • Reasonable • Can be "tough minded" • Fair—want everyone treated equally	• Guided by personal and social values • Assess impacts of decisions on people • Strive for understanding, harmony, and positive interactions • Compassionate • May appear "tenderhearted" • Fair—want everyone treated as an individual
JUDGING	**PERCEIVING**
• Scheduled • Organize their lives • Systematic • Methodical • Make short- and long-term plans • Like to have things decided • Try to avoid last-minute stress	• Spontaneous • Flexible • Casual • Open ended • Adapt; change course • Like things loose and open to change • Find last-minute pressures energizing

The four identified traits can come in sixteen different variations.

ISTJ	ISTP	ESTP	ESTJ
ISFJ	ISFP	ESFP	ESFJ
INFJ	INFP	ENFP	ENFJ
INTJ	INTP	ENTP	ENTJ

It's imperative for leaders to study and keep notes about all types to fully understand their team behaviors. Having this insight will expand your awareness and deliver all-inclusive support. It also helps avoid making common assumptions about staff—for instance, lack of motivation, lack of engagement, comprehension challenges, slow pace, lack of contribution, and inability to connect with the team. Unfortunately I have seen those who are the loudest and excited to volunteer and don't hesitate to give opinions get chosen for promotions or other benefits not because they were the best candidate but because they were the most noticeable and aligned with their leader's personality type, while some of the most talented individuals with unique styles were passed over. As a leader you want to make the best and fairest decision. Your team expects honesty, loyalty, and justice.

BENEFITS OF ESTABLISHING RELATIONSHIPS WITH YOUR TEAM

Instantly recognized as a fair, caring but powerful leader, your team will be honored to work with you and drive the mission! You will stand out and shine a light many will never forget. This will lead to relationships of longevity, even when some team members no longer work for your organization.

CONSEQUENCES OF NOT ESTABLISHING RELATIONSHIPS WITH YOUR TEAM

Team members will check out, only interested in their immediate needs. They will feel detached without having value. Be prepared for high turnover and poor productivity.

BEGIN BY

- Scheduling one-to-one meetings with each team member, accommodating their availability. Provide a nonintimidating messaging about the intent of the meeting mentioned above.

- Drafting questions and potential comments from your team members, developing responses to guide your conversations, and providing consistent messaging. Don't sound scripted, but be prepared. Remember that your team is always learning from you in good ways or bad. Good is better.

- Taking Myers-Briggs or any other gold standard training to understand all personality types.

- Reviewing your personality type from your test and determining your blind spots. This will help you identify personality types and automatically adapt to them. I challenge you to develop strategies to improve upon your support with team members who do not think and execute like you. This is also an opportunity for you to grow and gain more allies.

Be compelling and stand with integrity. Spend the time needed to get to know your team members one by one on both personal and professional levels. Know what makes them smile, panic, and push harder; what fascinates and discourages them; and what's significant to them at their core. I can't express how phenomenal this can be. During my many years as a leader, my greatest strength has come from developing valuable relationships with my team. I led and continue to lead by empowerment, listening to team members when they are facing death of loved ones, divorce, financial constraints, or marriage; graduating from college; welcoming babies; promoted to new roles; and much more. In all cases I treat them as a whole person, which allows me to handle them appropriately based on their work style and various events they are experiencing in all phases of life. They know they will not be left behind because they are a part of a work family that protects and honors them during their highs and lows!

Now that you understand how to connect with your team members both personally and professionally, you are equipped to provide effective role training.

CHAPTER 4

Provide Effective Role Training and Communication

Tell me and I forget, teach me and I may remember, involve me and I learn.

—BENJAMIN FRANKLIN

A

s a leader working with so many organizations across the country, I realized they all had one thing in common—prematurely concluding that most operational gaps are caused by staff mistakes, not following protocol. But what if the protocol is inadequate and not fulfilling its intended purpose? How can you hold your team accountable if they aren't efficiently trained? Leading health plan care management programs have many moving parts and a fair share of complexities. Recalling all the players is a challenge in itself; it's nothing short of exhaustive developing processes requiring frequent updating, integrated with the workflows of care managers, utilization reviewers, care management assistants, utilization intake specialists, benefits specialists, exercise physiologists, dietitians, social workers, pharmacists, respiratory therapists, team leads, managers, project managers, and directors.

I experienced this firsthand while leading a large care management transformation project, including a large healthcare organization with eleven facilities and over one thousand staff. My role during the implementation was to train care managers, utilization reviewers, and their assistants how to perform their roles based on changes their organization required to enhance their care management model. Before we could implement this work, we built a comprehensive training to walk through the organization's history, enterprise-wide metrics linked to regulatory compliance, growth initiatives, role of health plans/providers, and member outcome goals and then moved to building out detailed material. We made complex technical information easier for conception, incorporating step-by-step procedures for each role type, explaining what is required during the member healthcare journey phases when receiving medical/social services, as I mentioned in chapter 2. These phases again are as follows:

1. Member seeks treatment from provider.

2. Provider validates member insurance benefits and notifies plan of proposed treatment.

3. HP receives request for authorization or services from member or provider.

4. HP reviews for appropriateness and notifies provider and member of approved determination.

5. HP tracks utilization and quality of all services at all levels of care (e.g., inpatient, outpatient services) through discharge and ensures timely care transition notification.

6. UR sends care transition notification and referrals to HP care manager.

7. HP CM receives discharge notification and discharging facility documentation to begin the appropriate care transitions.

8. HP CM coordinates with entire healthcare team, including, but not limited to, PCP, specialists, hospital, skilled nursing facility, rehabilitation, long-term acute care, nursing home, medical supply vendor, and community organizations.

9. HP CM performs assessment and develops member care plan.

10. HP CM manages member care plan goals and interventions.

11. HP CM provides ongoing member support and follow-up.

This information was delivered in PowerPoint with manuals, associated job aids, articles, and white papers in formal classroom settings, one-to-one observations, focus groups, and self-paced electronic educational modules. I discovered that one tool was not any more effective than the other; using a combination of all at specific times was vital, although ongoing one-to-one observation with coaching was very instrumental to team members retaining information and allowed them to practice areas of opportunity.

What It Means to Provide Effective Role Training and Communication

Information is a source of learning, but if it is not organized, processed, and available to the right people in a format for decision-making, it is a burden, not a benefit. Creating standardization for compliance adoption, using leading practice methodologies, drafting policies/ procedures, mapping workflows, and facilitating onboarding/ongoing training are critical prior to delivering information to team members. It is also imperative to develop a governance plan identifying stakeholders in charge of operations and assigning specific roles and responsibilities to engineer execution, process improvement, and risk management, best illustrated through an organization chart symbolizing your organization's chain of command.

Information is a source of learning, but if it is not organized, processed, and available to the right people in a format for decision-making, it is a burden, not a benefit.

Training Plan Elements

COMMUNICATION AND CHANGE PLAN

Ineffective communication is a trend often experienced from the top down and the bottom up. It leads to errors in operational delivery; staff feeling confused, devalued, and frustrated; and decreased production.

As part of any training plan, clear and frequent communication must be the first order of business to prepare your organization, especially the operations team, for what's coming. They need to receive customized messaging about changes, business needs, and goals. It is helpful to understand various communication and change models and what will work best for your organization. Once a model is chosen, document communication and change activities. Consider examples below with anticipated staff reactions and recommendations to resolve.

THE CHANGE CURVE AND USAGE MODEL

Stage 1 – Individuals' initial response to change may be shock.
Recommendation: This is the most critical stage of communication. Provide clarity and answer questions in small doses.

Stage 2 – Negative response once reality of change is accepted (e.g., fear, perceived threats, anger) can lead to chaos.
Recommendation: Consider impacts and objections people may have, develop standardized messaging, plan to address concerns, and dispel myths from truth.

Stage 3 – Individuals start to let go of the old way and accept the changes, testing and exploring what the change means.
Recommendation: Develop and launch training in manageable components. It will take time for people to learn and execute the new process, and you can foster a healthy learning environment without punitive repercussions.

Stage 4 – Accept and embrace change fully.
Recommendation: Encourage discussions about successes and lessons learned; leverage for future projects.

LEWIN CHANGE MANAGEMENT MODEL

Stage 1 – Unfreeze (allow behavior, systems, and process change to happen)
Recommendation: Explain the need for change. Multiple and standardized communication methods are critical.

Stage 2 – Change (organization accepts change plan, transitioning to new way)
Recommendation: Ensure leaders and staff take an active role in changes.

Stage 3 – Refreeze (change fully adopted)

Recommendation: Manage consistency and monitor for reinforcements as needed.

BECKHARD AND HARRIS CHANGE EQUATION

This model states that for change to happen successfully, the following statement must be true:

Dissatisfaction × Vision × Practicality > Resistance to Change

Dissatisfaction – Your team must feel dissatisfied with the current situation before a successful change can take place. Without dissatisfaction, no one will likely feel very motivated to change. Communicate risks, issues, and impact if things remain the same.

Vision – The proposed solution must be attractive, and people need to understand what it is. If your team doesn't have a clear vision of what things will be like after the change and why things will be better, they probably won't be willing to work to deliver it. The clearer and more detailed you make this vision, the more likely it is that your team will agree with the change and move forward.

First Steps – Your team must be convinced that the change is realistic and executable. Allow them to help shape vision and participate in developing steps.

Resistance to Change – Resistance to change includes people's beliefs in the limits of the change, stubbornness toward any change, or lack of interest at the beginning.

By far the most effective method of dealing with resistance is to engage stakeholders in shaping the elements on the left side of the change equation. By involving stakeholders in assessing the need for change (dissatisfaction), creating a vision of a preferred future, and determining first steps toward achieving the vision, the system not only becomes richer in wisdom and passion but many real or potential concerns about the change will be addressed as well.

REQUIRED SECTIONS FOR COMMUNICATION AND CHANGE PLAN

COMPONENT	DESCRIPTION
Stakeholder/ Sponsorship Strategy	• Defines the framework for identifying, engaging, and supporting the sponsors throughout the transformation life cycle
Communication Strategy	• Identifies the approach for creating and delivering the right messages to the right people at the right time
Organization Design	• Identifies the skills/jobs required in the new model • Creates an organization structure designed to support process efficiency and standardization
Workforce Transition Management	• Maps retained and reallocated partners to the new/changed jobs and handles the people impact of the transition
Training and Performance Support	• Provides staff with the skills, knowledge, and support to perform the new staff processes in their new roles, using new/enhanced enabling technologies
Transition and Business Readiness	• Coordinates all go-live activities to transition processes
Culture and Branding	• Defines the strategic vision of transformation • Determines how to breed that mindset throughout your organization

Now that you understand how to communicate and prepare your team for change, it's time to deliver training composed of key content provided in multiple ways to engage and educate.

CLASSROOM

This type of training may be workshops to educate and teach large initiatives occurring across the organization impacting several team members like the care management transformation project mentioned above. Information is provided in presentation format with manuals and job aids to support learning. These sessions occur over several hours, usually one to two days, requiring the full attention of staff and temporary relinquishment of their daily roles and responsibilities. This is a significant investment from the organization, project sponsors, and executive leaders, so it is critical for the project team to develop comprehensive and effective training that will yield expected outcomes. For example, most team members should demonstrate newly acquired skills with the ability to execute competency within a specified time frame. Because this is delivery of a heavy amount of complex information, it is beneficial to create engaging material to keep your team members stimulated and awake!

Some things to avoid include the following:

- Not using icebreakers to introduce team members prior to presenting knowledge

- Reading slides verbatim with no context, like case studies, personal experiences, and hypothetical situations

- No variation in voice pitch; monotone delivery

- No group activities or knowledge checks to help with information retention and recall

- Not allowing questions during a presentation; by presentation close, the audience is ready to leave

All of these are real communication *killers*. It is important to understand the following: "The optimal attention span for an audience, i.e. the attention span that can be comfortably held by an interested human engaged in listening to a speaker, is not five to ten minutes. Instead, it is approximately twenty (20) minutes. In fact it is slightly less, somewhere in the 18-to-20 span, but twenty minutes is a decent and practical rough idea. Some people can hold their attention even longer, but they are outliers. After twenty minutes, no matter how interested we are, our focus is depleted, and will unless corrective action is taken erode steadily until we literally aren't listening any longer."[1]

Let's discuss how to avoid common blunders.

USE ICEBREAKER INTRODUCTION

Team members already have some reservations, possible resistance, fear, or competing priorities before attending your training presentation. The best way to help them let their guards down is by starting off with a fun, nonintimidating introduction of themselves. Asking everyone to mention their funniest moment, best vacation destination, favorite celebrity, or what animal they most identify with is a great way to do this. You will witness laughter, smiles, warmness, and automatic synergy before getting into intense material.

CREATE RICH POWERPOINT SLIDES

Know your audience and customize messaging and content to role groups:

- Executives are interested in facts supported by data. They will use information to make key product, financial, and growth

---

1   Alf Rehn, "The 20-Minute Rule for Great Public Speaking—On Attention Spans and Keeping Focus," Medium, April 11, 2016, https://medium.com/the-art-of-keynoting/the-20-minute-rule-for-great-public-speaking-on-attention-spans-and-keeping-focus-7370cf06b636.

strategy decisions. It is best to avoid granular detail; instead, bucket information in a few categories and use high-level language. Short, concise statements are best received.

- Middle management like managers and supervisors is focused on operations and staff performance status. They are expected to drive work execution and meet enterprise targets. It is best to provide group, aggregate-level information. Reference staff performance and operational summary reports.

- Frontline staff are engaged by role and responsibility information. Provide very detailed language at a task level. Reference workflows, policies, procedures, and training aides.

Organize content on slides into three main points with minimal narrative text. Rely on your talking points to elaborate in more detail. You don't want to lose your team members' attention with dense material or distract them with heavy information on the slides. The bulk of information should come from your words. Using examples and asking the audience questions were helpful in bringing clarity during many trainings I led. Don't be reserved—give them all you've got! The more they understand, the better chance of reaching competency and minimizing risk.

ALTERNATE VOICE PITCH

A monotone is a droning, unchanging tone. Nothing can put you to sleep more effectively than this. Try raising your pitch when emphasizing a topic or key point. Laugh when telling stories if appropriate. Be comfortable; think as if you are sitting in your living room, talking with loved ones or friends. Allow full transparency; be in the moment. Bring yourself into the presentation; individuals respond better to realness.

CONDUCT GROUP ACTIVITIES/ KNOWLEDGE CHECKS

We know adults have short attention spans and retain data better if presented in small chunks, so make sure each topic is discussed no longer than twenty minutes if possible. After each section jog their memory by asking two or three key questions referred to as "knowledge checks." This promotes participation and stimulates your team members' minds. It also alerts those who lost engagement to refocus.

Believe it or not, games work too. Some adults are still kids at heart (we should all hang on to our inner child!) and enjoy competitive games to showcase their knowledge, appreciating awards and prizes to recognize their achievement. You and your presenters should include at least one game to maintain engagement and have some much-needed fun to interrupt boredom. Some popular games that work well include Jeopardy!, Kahoot!, AhaSlides, and Wooclap. Make sure questions and answers are not too complicated; most team members should be able to answer all questions in a short period of time if engaged.

ALLOW QUESTION FLUIDITY

Although some presenters request questions at the end of the presentation based on time constraints, this is not the best method. Remember, retention is not easy; allowing someone to ask a question related to the current topic and providing a response is more effective. This will also stimulate the group to generate additional questions related to the same topic. Choose the best level of detail to produce clarity. Individuals feel more empowered when they can ask questions throughout a presentation without feeling restricted or that their thoughts are not prioritized. Questions are very healthy and demonstrate your team members are thinking and stimulated; optimize that moment while you have their attention. Don't be afraid of questions. Be prepared by anticipating what your team may ask and document and rehearse potential answers. If you don't know an answer, inform your team you will follow up within a specific time frame and do so.

Focused groups and just-in-time (JIT) training are other forms of classroom training. They are shorter in duration (around one hour) with smaller groups that can be more intimate. The goal is the same: to provide education and elicit feedback to influence how they deliver their roles and responsibilities. Focus groups usually include team members who have a vested interest in leading an effort and can be designed to train trainers to support their peers. All classroom settings use the same framework mentioned earlier.

One-to-One Observation/Coaching

This type of training is designed to provide individual support to team members after classroom training to further induce learning and retention. It allows trainers to witness execution and provide real-time coaching if opportunities are identified and to answer questions. It also involves validation, providing leaders more accurate findings to assess the progress of team learning and delivery of new or modified processes.

Self-Paced

Content is electronically loaded in a software application, usually a training platform with modules a team member can access at their leisure. Suggest adding any key training to allow team members to review. New team members hired after the event can gain the same learning as well. All training must be updated based on compliance mandate changes and process improvement initiatives.

Lastly, managing and monitoring performance is pivotal to measuring change adoption and execution of tasks from team members. Never take your eyes off the ship; losing ground will drastically impact success, lowering member quality, interrupting company growth, and decreasing profitability. Develop standardized competency tools with a built-in corrective action plan, evaluating all team member roles and responsibilities. Take caution using this approach too soon after training; allow team members to learn within an adequate amount of time before holding them accountable. As a leader it is understood that productivity is the bottom line, but remember, your team is like an extended family that trusts you and looks for fairness and protection as declared in chapter 3.

I cannot express enough the importance of adequate training; it's the foundation of any organization. How can team members be expected to perform roles and responsibilities without proper guidance during their employment? If you want to function like a quality-based center of excellence, it starts with you. The training blueprint you developed with others and provided to your team will help all of you reach organizational goals sprinkled with integrity and pride. Show them the way!

BENEFITS OF PROVIDING EFFECTIVE ROLE TRAINING AND COMMUNICATION

- Promotes clear role delineation. Staff will have no problem executing their responsibilities because you understand "a day in the life" of their role and help design sufficient workflows aligned with company metrics.

- Builds team confidence and increased job satisfaction. There's nothing like being empowered because you know what to do and how to do it.

- Creates an atmosphere of ongoing learning and growth.

- Supports standardization, making models and processes repeatable, reducing duplication of work, loss time, and productivity.

- Reveals your strength and expertise.

CONSEQUENCES OF NOT PROVIDING EFFECTIVE ROLE TRAINING AND COMMUNICATION

- Team role confusion. Team members will feel incompetence and shame, inspiring turnover and significant expenditure related to hiring and training new staff, replacing those who left your organization dissatisfied.

- Lack of standardization, a broken system that is convoluted and fragmented, and a toxic work environment that is impossible to exude dedication and value.

- Mistakes leading to member safety issues, compliance problems with penalties (e.g., suspension/termination of business), and poor reputation.

BEGIN BY

- Working with a team of project managers, training experts, consultants, and human resource leaders to brainstorm and build a training plan. Incorporate your industry expertise discussed in chapter 2 with a focus on compliance standards, leading practice training methodologies, staff feedback during whiteboarding sessions, and the latest technology tools.

- Making sure you have a heavy vetting process (prior to training going live) to comb through training, identify gaps, and tweak until it's at the level of satisfaction to truly evolve team members and result in change adoption, meeting your organization metrics and goals.

- Continuing to monitor training, document/share lessons learned, and modify as needed.

Take ownership and accountability for training; don't blindly pass this piece of work to others. Training and transparent communication is the key to running an organization. Enjoy experiencing seamless process flow, high productivity, happy work teams, and member satisfaction, all while serving a greater purpose than yourself. Remember, information is a source of learning; but unless it is organized, processed, and available to the right people in a format for decision-making, it is a burden, not a benefit.

After training team members, keep the growth fluid with proven development techniques for proposing career development opportunities.

CHAPTER 5

Propose Career Development Opportunities

The greatest leader is not necessarily the one who does the greatest things. Instead, the leader is the one that gets the people to the greatest things.

—RONALD REAGAN

The support and guidance I received from my manager, Corinne Crockett, at a large health plan still resonates with me today. I was a newly hired care manager with no experience, transitioning from a bedside charge nurse role, excited for the new position but nervous. I felt like I was at a disadvantage, not really familiar with managed care and the many tasks performed by care managers.

Although my manager led with a methodical, authoritative leadership style, she had a very protective and caring way about her. She was not hesitant to share my performance feedback, and her expectations aligned with our organization standards, but she met me where I was. She set up a customized training plan including frequent one-to-one meetings to evaluate my progress and had an open-door policy where I could ask questions any time. She always had encouraging words and saw greatness in me when I still felt like a fish out of water. She told me early in my tenure I was one of her strongest care managers with integrity, discipline, structure, and high-quality work, not distracted by others around me who did not display the same work ethic. She touched me when she said I interviewed the best out of all her candidates over her career. She also recognized strong potential and encouraged me to train newly hired staff, participate in mentorship programs, go back to school for an advanced degree, network with other peers and leaders in other departments, and consider leadership roles. She had the ability to see me beyond my current role and took time to develop my skills while sharing her personal and professional experiences.

A great leader is selfless and aims to push team members beyond their comfort zone so they can reach optimal capabilities.

She was more than a manager; she became my advocate, mentor, and friend. She was a major contributor to me moving into team lead and project manager positions at that health plan. I still remember her taking time, participating in mock interviews with me, helping me prepare for the interviews of these roles despite me no longer being under her leadership.

A great leader is selfless and aims to push team members beyond their comfort zone so they can reach optimal capabilities. They want to see you win throughout your entire career no matter where your path takes you!

What It Means to Propose Career Development Opportunities

Today's workforce is characterized by making multiple contributions to the organization via scrums, agile projects that are matched to the unique talent-sets that an individual brings. With career pathing, a concept of highlighting staff talents and aspirations to map further learning and employment opportunities, organizations' needs can more appropriately be matched with workers' desires. **—ADT**

We talked a great deal in the previous chapter about the importance of transparent, ongoing communication with your team and providing effective role training, which are both integral parts to career development. It is paramount to talk to your team daily, letting them know what is going on with your company vision, their role in helping reach that vision, acknowledging challenges you are facing, and listening to them coupled with effective training based on their personal work style.

But there are additional complimentary methods to foster growth, value, commitment, and longevity. Keep in mind that some individuals already know what they want to do, while others are still figuring things out. After getting to know your team and evaluating their performance over time, consider offering the following tools.

INTERNSHIP

This method is offered to students enrolled in an academic program; they are not your current team members, but there are benefits to your team. You can upskill your team members who are assigned to interns; they will learn how to plan, train, provide feedback, and lead an effort while exposing students to real-life projects and teaching them how to perform certain tasks to meet goals. This can also help build your candidate pool for entry-level positions with qualified individuals. Intern programs are most successful when the following are executed:

- Partner with academic programs to identify potential students.

- Select students from a diverse pool based on previously specified criteria and an equitable interview process.

- Develop performance goals that enhance the intern's skills and meet the organization's needs.

- Define responsibilities and a major project for the intern.

- Provide developmental feedback throughout the internship; share with the academic sponsor.

- Appropriately assign team members based on personality type, their goals, and their interest.

ROLE PROGRESSION SUPPORT/ SUCCESSION PLANNING

Making a lateral move or obtaining a promotion to learn and perform additional skills is a popular goal for many team members. They want to be mentioned in newsletters/staff meetings/announcements for their achievement, earn more money, make a lasting impact on an industry, make those closest to them proud, and feel like all their hard work in college and early career was worth it. Who better to prep them than a leader who knows their work style, performance, personality, and personal why? As a leader you are a coach designed to unlock hidden potential and maximize your team's performance by believing, encouraging, and developing. Develop a standardized approach to help team members advance to other positions. Make sure your plan includes the following:

- Helping team members determine their new role of interest and how it maps to their goals. Is it a good fit?

- Delivering tools to learn specific skills with added value beyond their current job description, enrolling in trainings/seminars/focus groups, assigning special projects to stretch their abilities.

- Monitoring and improving competency for new role requirements.

- Discussing organization needs, ensuring their promoted role expectations aligned with the bottom line.

- Regularly scheduled meetings to discuss progress, providing recommendations to reach goals as needed.

- Networking and introduction of team member to other leaders and key stakeholders, registering them for networking events.

- Providing ongoing encouragement.

MENTORING

The top benefits to organizations with formal mentoring programs are higher employee engagement and retention. Mentoring allows experienced staff to guide others through their career development journey and serve as an ongoing resource. Also, mentors themselves may experience greater internal satisfaction and fulfillment and a sense of rejuvenation in their role while also benefiting from the creativity, energy, and loyal support of their mentees. Mentees in a successful mentoring program may look forward to faster promotion rates, higher rates of career and pay satisfaction, and increased self-esteem.

It is also wise for leaders to follow ADDIE (analyze, design, develop, implement, and evaluate) guidelines in mentoring programs.

Ensure development and design is respectful of and in alignment with culture and organizational goals. Lastly, implement a plan that is thoughtfully marketed to ensure enthusiastic participation and include both formative and summative evaluation.

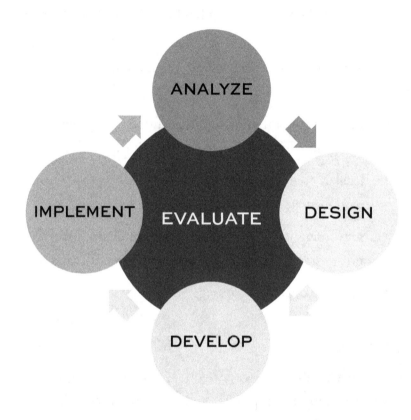

ELEMENTS FOR SUCCESS

1. Establish clear goals and objectives for the program.

2. Orient the participants so that both parties understand the purpose, needs, benefits, and expectations for the program and their respective roles, responsibilities, and qualifications.

3. Evaluate and match mentor personal characteristics, skills, and goals with the characteristics and needs of the mentees.

4. Provide interpersonal communication training and promote flexibility and tolerance for change for both parties.

5. Allow the mentor-mentee pair to work together on a trial or preparatory basis for a brief period.

6. Monitor, evaluate, and adjust throughout the entire mentorship relationship, focusing on both outcomes and process criteria.

BENEFITS OF PROPOSING CAREER DEVELOPMENT OPPORTUNITIES

- Leading a high-performing team with abilities to enhance and evolve your organization business strategies

- Acknowledgment of exceptional delivery and being a role model for other leaders

- Most importantly, satisfied staff with dedication

CONSEQUENCES OF NOT PROPOSING CAREER DEVELOPMENT OPPORTUNITIES

- Missed opportunity to grow team members and have qualified candidates for future roles

- Team members leaving your organization for others with better developmental opportunities

BEGIN BY

- Developing a standardized plan

- Meeting with team members to discuss their goals and interest for promotions and lateral moves

- Implementing the plan for specific team members

- Continuing to evaluate your plan and make changes as needed to improve

A boundless leader does more than manage daily staff activities to meet productivity; they understand the value of team development, bringing the best out of them so they are not only a great worker but also an evolved human being who will leave a lasting impression.

Now that you understand how to develop your teams, let's move to learning how to promote team autonomy and accountability.

CHAPTER 6

Promote Team Autonomy and Accountability

The autonomy of the individual appears to be complemented and enhanced by the movement of the group; while the effectiveness of the group seems to depend on the freedom of the individual.

—HAKIM BEY

Building a culture in which people take accountability to deliver on its promises is hard work and can be difficult to accomplish. Only when every person is held accountable to themselves, their peers, and their shared possibility can the impossible become possible.

—GINGER GRAHAM

I was twenty-four years old and terrified. I had just completed five years of demanding nursing curriculum with high-level expectations and daily pressure to perform. At a basic level, I was worried about not being able to perform the duties of a registered nurse in a fast-paced surgical/orthopedic unit. On top of that, people's lives depend on our skills and decisions. Job stress doesn't get much worse than that. To me it is similar to being a military soldier or police officer, where you often have to make specific choices, many times under great duress, and sometimes those choices impact or take another's life.

My nursing education was solid, and I cannot thank my university enough for its rigorous preparation, but it wasn't sufficient to calm my nerves and give me full confidence to trust my instincts that I could prevent unsafe practices, provide robust disease education to patients, and perform high-risk procedures like blood transfusions, wound care, insertion of intravenous apparatus and nasogastric tube, chest tube maintenance, breathing machine management, and administering potent IV medications that could be life threatening if a patient had an allergic response. For example, incorrectly handing a chest tube could cause a collapsed lung, patients might have allergic reactions to medication, and my first exposure to breathing machines and respirator application made me nervous—like giving a speech in front of my sixth-grade class.

Making matters worse, my fear was exacerbated by micromanagement and excessive authority from my direct supervisor, also a nurse, who took me under her wing and guided my daily responsibilities. I remember feeling so paralyzed and intimidated that I could barely perform tasks I excelled at in my nursing curriculum. My supervisor watched everything I did and constantly berated me when I did not do something in a way she preferred. It was not necessarily an incorrect action on my part; it just wasn't the way she did it and her choice in how to direct her team. I struggled to maintain confidence. I dreaded going to work every day and eventually left the organization with less than one year of employment. It was an unfortunate situation for both parties directly inspired by that experience.

What It Means to Promote Team Autonomy and Accountability

In a CareerAddict.com article, Chris Leitch explains how micromanaged staff is ineffective and results in passive-aggressive behavior, feeling of incompetence, stress, and an overall unhealthy working environment.[2] The inability to delegate work and empower team members to act with autonomy is one of the quickest ways to alienate them. I truly believe most leaders want to avoid this but face common challenges and need guidance to resolve them. Some challenges include the following.

STRESS

Imagine the challenge of completing the nursing curriculum and clinicals. You are filled with confidence and excitement for a new and fulfilling career, and then COVID-19 hits. Nurses take an oath to care for people, and we know risks are always present, but now there's a deadly virus circling the globe, killing many thousands of people every day, and you're exposed to it every time you go to work. In addition to everyday job demands, you face the added stress of contracting a virus that you could take back to your loved ones.

The COVID-19 pandemic heavily impacted medical facilities and staff around the world, including seasoned nurses, new graduates, and frontline-tested managers with decades of experience. COVID-related stress rocketed to barely manageable levels, and in fact, many nurses and their leaders reached a breaking point and left the field altogether. You never want to be in a position to choose which patient

---

2   Chris Leitch, "The Devastating Effects of Micromanagement," CareerAddict, February 11, 2016, https://www.careeraddict.com/the-devastating-effects-of-micromanagement.

is "worse off" than the one in the next bed and gets the breathing machine while the other dies.

Additionally, micromanaging tells team members that their judgment isn't trusted, and when team members don't feel trusted, they don't work to their highest potential.

It is a dreadful scenario, and when involved leaders, already saddled with demands and expectations, feel like they don't have a good handle on things, they tighten their grip on everything, often killing creativity, driving down performance, and causing mental instability for their team and themselves. All creative ideas come from a unique place. They are untested and might even seem foolish, but if your grip on operations is too tight to allow for experimentation, creativity will surely dissolve. Additionally, micromanaging tells team members that their judgment isn't trusted, and when team members don't feel trusted, they don't work to their highest potential. Build off your self-awareness, review your personality type and associated stressors, and have a self-awareness game plan to tackle as we discussed in chapter 1.

LACK OF LEADERSHIP TRAINING

Far too many leaders, in all industries, are not satisfied in their work and are disengaged, and low productivity is a common refrain. According to the Association for Talent Development (ATD), disengaged leaders cost $300 billion in lost productivity, 65 percent of leaders are disengaged at work, and 62 percent of leaders aren't given critical skills to succeed.[3] Just as direct reports need adequate training, so do leaders. Unfortunately many organizations do not have a formal training for managers, directors, or senior leadership. You are expected to know it all on day one and hit the ground running based on your previous experience.

Although many leaders have a strong academic and performance history, they still require proper onboarding, a transition plan, collaboration with other key leaders, and ongoing training, mentoring, and support. It needs to be structured with one or more people assigned to you to help get a handle on the current state of things and what is expected. A new leader can't fix everything on the first day; impacting productivity is a four- or five-month process, establishing relationships with key people and getting to know your colleagues.

I rarely received adequate training when I progressed to leadership roles; I had to do my own assessment and develop a plan, then discuss my needs with my direct manager. I was able to prevent myself from drowning and eventually reached sustainability, but the burden should never be on the employee to figure out alone. As a leader you will benefit from discussing training and transition plans prior to executing your work and ensure you get what you need to be successful.

NOT KNOWING YOUR TEAM

In chapter 3 we discussed at length the positive effects of knowing your team both personally and professionally—what drives their motivation, immediate goals, career interest, unique ideas, and work style based on a personality test. If this step is skipped, it results in

---

3   Tomika Greer, "The Essentials of a Talent Development Internship," *TD*, March 2, 2020, https://www.td.org/magazines/td-magazine/the-essentials-of-a-talent-development-internship.

lack of trust between you and your team. It is not surprising if you aren't comfortable with giving them a range of freedom because you don't know them, but once again, meet with your team members, talk with them, listen to them, and most importantly keep your promise to treat them like an extended family.

LOW PRODUCTIVITY RELATED TO INADEQUATE TEAM TRAINING

When a team is not well trained, low-quality work and decreased performance leading to missed targets and metrics is inevitable. As mentioned in chapter 4, training is the foundation. If team members don't know what to do and how to do it, they can't meet performance expectations. They are defeated and confused and lack confidence, and leaders can't see the way to autonomy. Ensure your team is trained, and you will get over this hurdle.

Leaders who own up to their slipups influence teams to take ownership of mistakes.

Now let's talk about accountability, the successor of training and autonomy. Before we discuss team expectations, think about this: leaders who own up to their slipups influence teams to take ownership of mistakes. No one is perfect. Although a lot of time and effort is exhausted to learn industry trends, process delivery, and ways to mitigate risks, things can still go wrong, even with the best of intentions. As a leader I worked with my teams to establish process improvement techniques, which seemed great in theory and on paper, but once executed, they failed and had to be revamped. I discussed with my team areas I missed, taking my own ownership and accountability. It was amazing to witness them do the same, and they told me not to be so hard on myself and that we all were in it together.

Don't underestimate the power of honesty and transparency. Remember, as a leader you are leading by example and viewed as a role model. Holding yourself accountable and providing effective training and guidance makes it easier for your team to own their results. You want to use efficient tools and standardize the way you measure competency, delivering consistent feedback to your teams. The best way to do this is by developing or using leading practices:

- Responsible, accountable, consulted, and informed (RACI) grids that illustrate roles and responsibilities. This is a simple way to display the expectations of all your team roles. It further shows restricted tasks to a particular role versus those shared, requiring two-way directional responsibility and communication. Provide this to your new team members and provide updates as processes change.

- Competency templates to evaluate and monitor your team roles and responsibilities. You will have the capability to streamline key tasks and apply a weighted measure, for example, B for basic knowledge level requiring a lot of prompting, I for intermediate knowledge level with adequate understanding and independence, and E for expert level with advanced knowledge, significant independence, and minimal prompting, if any. Having a good view of where your team stands with consistent measures gives you critical insight to develop remediation plans to help team members improve upon opportunities. This also leaves no surprises to your team during performance and end-of-year evaluations.

- Role and responsibility scorecard aligned with organizational metrics. This should sync up to the competency spreadsheet above. It's very helpful to teams when they understand how their individual work rolls into enterprise-wide targets, and it also shows them how important their work is on a larger scale, inspiring an increase in investment and commitment.

- Team meetings to discuss role expectations, the tools used above, and how they will be measured. Adjust frequency based on newly launched initiatives requiring close monitoring and those that are routine (e.g., weekly, biweekly, or monthly).

A thorough approach to managing your team competency while giving them freedom results in a high-performing, motivated team with impeccable confidence. Performance management discussions should not be a time of fear and nail biting for your teams; expectations should be clear and fair.

BENEFITS OF PROMOTING TEAM AUTONOMY AND ACCOUNTABILITY

A strong, cohesive, and passionate team is ready for any challenge that comes their way. Why? Because they have a leader who respects and trusts them, a solid training to efficiently complete their roles and responsibilities, healthy relationships with one another, and clear expectations of daily tasks so they can take ownership.

CONSEQUENCES OF NOT PROMOTING TEAM AUTONOMY AND ACCOUNTABILITY

A team with no sureness feels suffocated and paralyzed, not trusting anything they do with the fear of being reprimanded. Nothing can be unhealthier than this. When teams are lost and in despair, they will eventually leave your organization, but prior to that, you will experience a hit in productivity because they are distracted and don't feel their work is worthy, so why bother?

BEGIN BY

- Doing a self-check on your mood, evaluating your stress level, identifying triggers such as competing deadlines, correcting mistakes you did not make, and accommodating others' work styles. Resolve as best as you can and always refer to your personality type test. Without application it will be of no use.

- Ensuring you have what you need to perform your role, especially operation compliance training, to understand how your department should run aligned with accreditation and quality standards. Also, it is critical to learn effective ways to communicate with your stakeholders, teams, external vendors, and senior leadership. Other key areas include taking personal accountability, staying engaged, increased listening, and assessing.

- Continuing to treat your team as your extended family, protecting them, building trust, advocating for them, serving as a guide, and setting clear expectations regarding their role and responsibility targets/metrics. Be flexible, willing to hear them out when mistakes happen, and make modifications to processes if more suitable.

- Using leading practice competency tools. Walk through with your team and explain how they will be measured and the evaluation frequency; set up regularly scheduled meetings for feedback and well checks.

Lack of freedom to express their individualism, share their vision, make decisions, and discover how their unique gifts can support your organization will stunt your team's growth and lead to discontent. How can they even imagine taking ownership? Don't be afraid to loosen your grip if you hired qualified talent, built a rapport, trained effectively, and supported the development of your team. Let smart people do what they do best—thrive. They don't require being overly managed!

Now that your teams are going above and beyond to provide quality member services, functioning like a well-oiled machine and center of excellence, it's time to give them all the praise and recognition they deserve. In our next chapter, we will walk through different ways to honor to your diverse team.

CHAPTER 7

Show Praise and Appreciation

There is more hunger for love and appreciation in this world than for bread.

—MOTHER TERESA

"Tramico, you are an excellent nurse who provides exemplary service to our members. I consider you a privilege to our condition care team." These words from my previous manager and similar accolades from college professors, team members, and close friends about my personal and professional attributes never leave my mind. Sentiments like this, uttered from the heart with sincerity, reach the deepest part of us and support moments when we question our purpose and actions. In times like these, we often look for clarity about who we truly are and what we represent, while pondering the next steps during a life transition attributed to values and principles revolutionized through family tradition, scholars, mentors, or unity practices.

This can be a difficult ask, especially when daily life is uprooted in times like the COVID-19 pandemic, which brought out people's frustrations and, in many instances, divided families, communities, and entire populations. Even in the best of times, we are all affected by society's trappings, and as a leader, this is when to show your best side, step up, and show your team the love and attention they deserve.

Team members value your opinion, leaving you in a unique position to acknowledge their work effort and character, which they will remember for a long time.

When I evaluate my career, it's not based on money I earned but by the lives I impacted. I go to a quiet place without distractions, reminiscing on feedback from past managers with whom I have a close bond and praises from peers, direct reports, and members and indulging in certificates, emails, cards, internal newsletters, and recommendations. There is nothing more blissfully energizing than to reflect and know that, despite obstacles, your journey was beneficial because of your efforts. You realize you are permanently imprinted in sand that will not wash away. You are and will be remembered!

In the healthcare field, there is no comparable dollar amount to what you do. You're there because you want to make a difference in the world, and team members value your opinion, leaving you in a unique position to acknowledge their work effort and character, which they will remember for a long time. It costs you nothing but will lead to a fortune.

What It Means to Show Praise and Appreciation

Your team looks up to you and values your opinion. They want to perform at a high level and not leave you disappointed in their work while meeting targeted goals. As such, values-based recognition programs should contribute significantly to your organization's key metrics, including engagement, retention, safety, and wellness. Programs must be authentic and personalized to increase team member engagement and retention by avoiding generic gifts (e.g., giving everyone the same certificate), top-down organizational process, and perception that the process is political.

Appreciation is showing gratitude and giving recognition to someone for something. Imagine what it felt like when you were recognized for an achievement. Did you feel happy? Did you feel valued? Did you get a warm and fuzzy feeling inside? Were you filled with excitement, ready to burst the good news to those who are important to you? I am sure you can relate since leaders invest a lot into themselves through completion of multiple academic programs, job trainings, and participation in professional groups, leading to countless achievements in the workplace and community. As you reflect on your positive memories, imagine what your team members will experience if you spread appreciation and praise to them, recognizing their contributions with specific callouts and related presentations. For example, selecting an employee of the month should go beyond simply handing that person a template certificate on their lunch break; make it real with genuine appreciation for a particular accomplishment or consistent high-level performance.

Keep in mind that leaders can express recognition in various ways to appeal to their diverse team, but it is important to understand that compensation is not the driving force for everyone. I walked away from an organization shortly after a $30,000 promotion due to lack of appreciation for my hard work. This field has never been about money for me, and most of my colleagues will agree—we are motivated to help others.

Prior to deciding which type of recognition is best, go back to your staff personality type summaries. Review what is important to them and recall conversations you had during one-to-one meetings— their values, principles, what makes them wake up every day with intentions to be their best selves. I once led a team of twenty care managers for a small chronic condition care organization. They were all women and mostly leaders of their families, taking care of their kids or aging parents and helping other family members. Many were overwhelmed, constantly saying there was not enough time in a day to complete all their work and personal things. "If I could just have a day off to catch up on appointments or even a flexible schedule. I don't want to leave this job. I like my team, but it seems impossible to fit it in with all I have to do at home." I heard them loud and clear and worked with executive leadership to develop a recognition program to include paid time off prizes and flexible scheduling options to boost their engagement and help avoid high turnover.

This is just one example of genuinely knowing your team, their challenges, and tailoring recognition to maintain enthusiasm for their roles. Positive, motivated team members are far more likely to stay with an organization for many productive years and often for their entire careers.

Ways to Appeal to Your Team Members

1. **Verbal Praise.** Although it may seem simple, stopping at the work space of your team member, asking him/her to come to a private location, setting up a phone call to acknowledge high-quality process delivery in alignment with company standards, or calling out a characteristic that positively

impacted your department like resilience, compassion, self-motivation, flexibility, creativity, patience, honesty, or loyalty will give your team member reassurance and confidence. It does not necessarily need

Team members trust feedback provided privately and coming from the heart as opposed to hearing it in front of a group.

to be a grandiose, dramatic display; a lot of times, a heartfelt comment or pat on the back for something they did that had a positive impact goes a long way. This works because team members trust feedback provided privately and coming from the heart as opposed to hearing it in front of a group. Remember that while some of your team members revel in glory from the attention of a crowd, many do not prefer this.

2. **Awards/Certificates.** Awards are common and well received in our society, understood as receiving acknowledgment of merit for excellence in a field, sports, or academics. To have the most impact, leaders should make awards specific and avoid general language, for example, labeling an award as an impact award for quality member service with safe outcome as opposed to a departmental impact award. Awards are usually announced during staff meetings or in front of a collective audience, but if you recognize a team member who does not take compliments in stride or shies away from crowds and is more comfortable with one-to-one communication, it is best to ask if it's okay to share before making a grand declaration. In fact, research shows 30 to 40 percent of employees say they are uncomfortable placed in front of a group to receive an award.

3. **Paid Time Off.** Busy schedules with unexpected life changes, competing deadlines, everyone expecting something from you all at once, hardly a moment to take a breath—this is our reality these days, and I don't know anyone who would turn down a paid time off award for doing something great at work. As I mentioned in an earlier example, when my leadership team offered this benefit to our care managers, many of them could not believe it and were honored to receive such a gift. They mentioned it was exactly what they needed to spend a day for self-care, catch up on errands, spend time with family or loved ones, or just do nothing. The opportunity to recover from stress and challenges and reset is a tremendous leap toward team members being fulfilled at work and contributing in consistently impactful ways.

4. **Peer-to-Peer Recognition.** We mentioned several times in this book that work teams are like an extended family and that everyone has a role to play. The opinion of all members is highly respected and desired, especially from peers. They are the boots on the ground, work closely together every day, and are good evaluators of how work tasks should be done. Who better to evaluate your work than your peers? You depend on one another; whether a team member is a strong performer or not, the team feels it, and they never hesitate to hold each other accountable so things run smoothly. When I worked the front lines and everyone was working hard on high-stress days, the last thing I wanted was a sloppy handoff of shift responsibilities that adds more headache to a coworker. You can feel the heat from those you work with, and it makes you feel accountable. On the other hand, a team working well together is equally generous with recognizing top-shelf work.

Industry best practice is to have a process in place for team members to acknowledge each other, for example, nominating others for awards, employee of the month, prizes, or other scenarios, including a reason for the recommendation. Team members exchanging verbal accolades, pats on the back, or private, shared praise should be encouraged.

5. **Flexible Scheduling.** We have learned over the years that work schedules are not "one size fits all" and that more hours worked don't necessarily equate to more work being done. I witnessed team members who worked eight hours with lower productivity than those who worked six hours. Keep in mind that based on the industry and nature of work, there are peak times for productivity, such as 10:00 a.m. to 6:00 p.m. compared with 8:00 a.m. to 4:00 p.m. This should give you a range to consider flexible scheduling for your high performers as a means of appreciation for their dedication and contributions to your organization's key performance measures.

6. **Organizational Announcement.** Some of your team members can't wait to be showcased in front of their peers and leaders, and that's okay. They want others to know they are a team player, strive for service excellence, and possess unique talents. Include them in newsletters, company-wide emails, internal intranet pages, or any forum with a large audience.

7. **Promotion/Bonus.** Team members who express interest in development and growth and followed your career path coaching and recommendations should be considered for a promotion with enhanced roles and responsibilities and

higher pay if available in your organization. Based on your performance reviews and one-to-one meetings, there should a commensurate salary increase as well. I've seen some organizations promote team members with minimal pay increase or none if it was a lateral move. In cases like this, you will lose the engagement of team members who prefer compensation awards. Learning and executing new skills with proficiency takes commitment and discipline; ensure they receive what they deserve.

8. **Team Celebration.** Coming from a consulting background, team dinners, holiday gatherings, and team building events were always crowd-pleasers. If your team helped your organization obtain new/extended contracts, impress a client, meet/exceed yearly performance guarantees, or show resilience during a tough year filled with frequent changes, societal challenges, or unexpected growth requiring long work hours, plan a group celebration. "Hey, let's get together and celebrate the recent client milestone." Who doesn't love events like that? Before diving in, however, get insights from your team members regarding preferences for the event venue, formality/informality, food/drink, and other details.

9. **Point System Award.** In recent years many companies experienced success with point system awards, where points are earned by team members and used for a gift of preference as opposed to management handing out generic, neutral gifts that don't appeal to everyone. Points are obtained from metric performance, leader or peer nominations, good attendance records, or any other values of importance to your organization. Team members build points to choose a gift of

their preference and can sometimes donate points to other team members.

10. **Gifts and Goodies.** Giving low-cost monetary gifts like gift cards are always well received by team members, as is breakfast, lunch, or desserts. Food is a common dominator for happiness—morning doughnuts, bagel breaks, Friday pizzas, catered lunches. Everyone likes to eat, especially your foodie team members.

BENEFITS OF GIVING PRAISE AND RECOGNITION

Now more than ever, teams need to feel genuinely appreciated from the heart. Don't think twice about saying, "You are doing a fantastic job providing comprehensive education to our members, and they are receiving you well based on our member surveys" or "I know society seems to be chaotic at the moment, but I appreciate your commitment to our team. If you want to discuss anything, I am here for you." It only takes a few seconds to say motivating, kind words, and it goes a long way with your team members. Use various methods to stimulate them; you know who they are, what they like, and what they value. Imagine how you will shock them because you took the time to understand uniquely who they are and give purposeful praise. This will dramatically build their trust and admiration.

CONSEQUENCES OF NOT GIVING PRAISE AND RECOGNITION

Bitter, disengaged, and disconnected team members feel like they are machines used for productivity only. Providing feedback on areas they need to improve will not be well received; it's hard to receive that type of information if they never hear what they are doing well. They will assume everything is negative, become disconnected, hold resentment, and harbor no desire to function at their highest potential. In some cases a team member might develop inclinations to leave the organization or develop an attitude of "I'm only here because I need a paycheck" versus "I want to build a career with this great team and want my manager to be proud of me."

BEGIN BY

- Evaluating all team members' performance and character. Identify individuals who made a difference, went above and beyond, improved from previous performance, and overcame obstacles.

- Giving customized praise and recognition based on their preferences. Remember to ask team members if it is okay to make public announcements about their accolades.

- Not just giving recognition quarterly or at scheduled intervals. Do it spontaneously to surprise your team members and prevent them from thinking the process is only political.

We are approaching the finish line to functioning as a responsible and influential leader. Let's look closer at continuing process monitoring and improvement.

CHAPTER 8

Continue Process Monitoring and Improvement

The most dangerous phrase in the English language is "we have always done it this way."

—DR. GRACE HOPPER

Y ou can't do what you've always done if what you've always done isn't working. I realized the significance of process improvement to maintain sustainability during my years of supporting various healthcare organizations. Keeping high-performing teams, streamlined workflow, innovative technology with ease of use, data-driven reporting, and safe practices is a lot to handle and can't be accomplished without constantly monitoring operational processes and the workflow of team members.

In one scenario I joined a project to identify and understand the root cause of process gaps and help create solutions to improve business flow. It was apparent, although the project was underway for several months, that a standardized approach to evaluate how client deliverables were modified, reviewed for quality, finalized, and submitted to clients was absent. The deliverables were very important, with specific requirements aiding a very large, expensive, and time-sensitive initiative with outcomes expected to prevent life-threatening member events. This is, of course, potentially disastrous. Unmet healthcare expectations leave people's lives at risk and questions the intentions of the entire project.

What It Means to Continue Process Improvement and Monitoring

The most comprehensive and strategic method to evaluate your operations and correct anything resulting in unsafe member experiences, sluggish productivity, decreased revenue, compliance issues, and stunted growth is to work with a dedicated team of experienced leaders to perform an assessment of your operations department's current state. Assessments are gold standard, involving deep evaluation of all delivery requirements and associated tasks performed by every role type with a focus on people, process, and technology. When undertaking process improvement, it must be done methodically, mapping back to a working model to evaluate current operations and overcome obstacles such as sluggish productivity or compliance issues.

ASSESSMENT COMPONENTS

Step 1: Speak with team members who represent each role type, such as nurses, administrative assistants, and pharmacists. It is critical to understand what's going on during collaboration and integration points between the teams and cross-functional departments. Know what is happening with tasks requiring integration and handoff. Get a pulse check on how they are performing key processes and review what's working well and opportunities for improvement. Keep in mind that leaders are often not expected to do this on their own. They should bring in key people from the organization, including consultants, fellow leaders, and project managers. Document findings to stay abreast of potentially serious problems. This is a time to be objective and recognize themes across process concerns, role confusion, and technology challenges. Prior to asking team questions, build their trust, and inform them that their comments are confidential and will only be communicated collectively in categories and that their names are not tied to anything.

Step 2: Review and analyze operational workflows, policies, program descriptions, compliance plans, job descriptions, competency tools, staffing models, system implementation requirements, data, and reports to identify any gaps related to compliance, operational flow, productivity, and member safety. Is everything in sync? Are processes following prescribed protocol? Are policies and procedures updated to reflect protocols? Does the team understand new processes or changes?

The best way to identify gaps is to compare the current functionality of operational tasks to a list of foundational capability requirements, what is referred to as a baseline tracker. It can be broken out by program subgroups—chronic care management, behavioral health, maternity, complex care, quality/compliance, transition of care, utilization management, and appeals—mapped to member journey phases, including steps performed by all role types. Create a separate tab with a list of system foundational capabilities. Rate gaps as "low impact" if member safety or compliance is not at risk; score "moderate" or "critical" for gaps caused by noncompliance with CMS, NCQA, URAC, or contractual requirements; member facing adverse events from gaps in care by health plan or provider; revenue loss; or decreased expansion.

Keep in mind that leaders should not be expected to memorize a twenty-page policy, but they should know it's there and its key points.

Step 3: Develop leading practice solutions to resolve gaps; work with advanced team members, consultants, and other leaders to develop methods aligned with contractual requirements, regulatory agencies, and models approved by industry experts, generally used by center of excellence organizations. This piece of work entails time; it can't be rushed and demands a thorough approach. Conduct several whiteboard sessions; analyze pros and cons, bearing in mind how changes will impact roles and responsibilities, system capabilities, and type of training required.

Step 4: Build out a road map for preimplementation, implementation, and postimplementation activities, including an effective change and communication plan, customizing information for frontline, middle management, and executive leaders at specific time periods. Timelines need to be realistic, allowing team members to learn new roles and responsibilities comfortably prior to delivery. Refer to chapter 4 for further details.

Step 5: Implement new or enhanced processes in your going-live plan with structure and standardization. As a reminder, change adoption takes approximately thirteen months, so close monitoring and reinforcement is best for optimal success.

There are times a full assessment may not be necessary, especially if your department had one recently. You may be already aware of a few processes requiring tweaking based on your observations and communication from frontline staff, team leads, managers, and cross-functional departments like enrollment, benefits, appeals, claims, and provider networking. In this case develop solutions with support and feedback from selected team members, other leaders, and possibly consultants to develop communication messaging, training, and monitoring plans similar to the above recommendations.

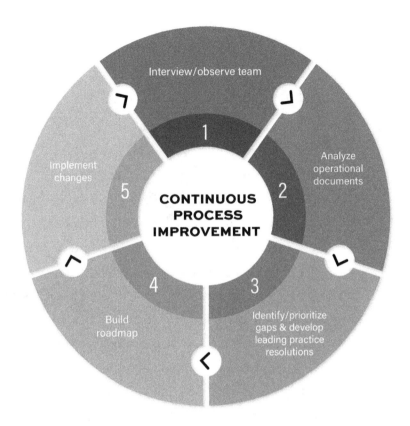

Most importantly remember that email is not the only way to communicate critical updates. People get lost in it, and you have a lot of work on your hands if you have multiple department heads and team leads. Go and talk with them, host a meeting or focus group, or pull together a luncheon or town-hall-type gathering. Be sure your team knows you don't expect them to just know everything and go do it; give them what they need and train them accordingly.

Be sure your team knows you don't expect them to just know everything and go do it; give them what they need and train them accordingly.

As you gear up to find barriers to operational delivery, be aware of some common HP gap trends. Having this knowledge will allow you to promptly target critical areas.

PEOPLE/PROCESS

1. **Lack of integration between care management internal team members—for example, UR and CM.** As mentioned in chapter 2, when internal team members do not effectively communicate key information and data for a member health history and previous involvement in other health plan programs during a transition, this leads to missed opportunities for a proper health assessment and care planning. The member may not receive appropriate referrals to internal and external programs or coaching to address areas of need. Tighten up handoff steps with corrective action for team members. Alignment with system enhancements will improve data exchange between UM and CM team members.

2. **Limited integration between care management team members, external providers, and vendors.** Also discussed in chapter 2, some vendors are contracted to provide member wellness education, PCP/specialist request procedures and services, home health agencies provide in-home nursing care, and supply companies deliver critical supplies like oxygen, just to name a few. When there is a gap in communication and poor follow-up, members are at increased risks for health crises and unfavorable events, like medication errors, delayed treatment, overlap in communication from various

team members, and duplicate services. Align processes with enhanced system integration and work with team members to understand how to appropriately coordinate with providers and vendors; include time frames, scripted messaging, and escalation pathways.

3. **Inconsistent training resulting in poor process delivery.** We talked about this quite a bit earlier in the book. Sufficient training is key to any care management program success. Team members need to know why they are doing what they are doing and how. If not, they will experience role confusion, incompetence, or shame and potentially walk off the job. In addition, as a leader you will further experience lack of standardization, a broken system, toxic work environment, mistakes leading to member safety issues, compliance problems with penalties (e.g., suspension/termination of business), and poor reputation. Review chapter 4 for training ideas.

TECHNOLOGY/DATA

4. **Care management technology system minimally supports full integration.** CMS Interoperability and Patient Access final rule and compliance is a newly launched mandate requiring HPs and providers to improve their overall system capabilities with a focus on interfaces between various platforms and bidirectional data exchange and increase data submission frequency. The goal is a future where data flows freely and securely between HPs, providers, and members to achieve truly coordinated care, improved health outcomes,

and reduced costs. As mentioned previously in Chapter 2 some elements include the following:

⇒ Medicaid managed care plans and CHIP managed care entities to comply with a beneficiary's (member's) request to have their health data transferred from HP to HP, including encounter data, clinical information, and authorization status

⇒ To exchange certain data with CMS daily on beneficiaries (members) who are dually eligible for Medicaid and Medicare for improved accuracy

⇒ To design, develop, install, or enhance claims processing and information retrieval systems to meet regulatory expectations

⇒ Integrated approach to ensure access to covered services consistent with requirements and to coordinate and promote optimal utilization of healthcare resources; make utilization decisions that affect the healthcare of beneficiaries (members) in a fair, impartial, and consistent manner; and assist with transition to alternative care when benefits end, should an enrollee no longer be eligible for benefits

The new changes involve a huge work effort; collaborate with technical and business project teams to ensure mandates are followed.

5. **Care management technology system rule engines not customized with compliance requirements.** There are many times when HP systems are missing configured rule engines including auto assignment, auto referrals with loop closure,

auto notifications for actions to meet quality measures, hard stops for assessment/care plan timely submissions, authorization and time stamps aligned with federal/state programs, HP unique book of business, and specialized populations. Work closely with data analysts, health information management, and IT department leaders to resolve issues.

6. **Underutilized system capabilities.** There are several inactivated features due to training gaps, limited resources for configuration, and customization request. Ensure features are turned and set governance around the change request process. Changes should only be allowed after seeking leadership permission.

7. **Variable reporting.** Several systems lack ad hoc reporting for tracking and monitoring success of member-centric internal and external programs, member program outcomes, service-level agreements, performance guarantee, and member-level incentives by defined groups or business units with active benefit summary tables within the system. Again, work with data analysts, health information management, and IT department leaders to resolve issues.

BENEFITS OF CONTINUING PROCESS MONITORING AND IMPROVEMENT

- Less risks and issues

- Equipped with a game plan to evaluate operational process through a standardized method, including use of baseline tracker to quickly identify gaps, scheduled quality checks, dedicated team to brainstorm and come up with leading practice solutions, and robust training with various learning options and successful delivery, resulting in high-quality members services, high productivity, compliance, increased revenue, and growth aligned with your organization metrics

CONSEQUENCES OF NOT CONTINUING PROCESS MONITORING AND IMPROVEMENT

- Several process mistakes from team members, who may develop work-arounds not necessarily better or standardized

- Duplication of work, decreasing productivity

- Inconsistent performance across team members

- Not meeting enterprise-wide targets and client guarantees, failing external quality audits

- Possible regulatory penalties, suspension of health plan, reduced members

BEGIN BY

- Determining if you need a full assessment or not. If you do, select a team, including middle managers, directors, and industry consultants if possible.

- Identifying key gaps using leading practice tools to compare functionality with foundational requirements like a baseline tracker.

- Developing solutions and test various possibilities. Keep in mind how they will impact system capabilities and team member roles.

- Documenting lessons learned.

Conclusion

Every leader is a manager, but not every manager is a leader.

—TRAMICO HERMAN

L eadership is not the path for everyone. It requires both natural and learned qualities with a significant amount of selfless respon- sibility, much different from what you may have witnessed on your current or prior career path. As a matter of fact, the deeper you fall into the leadership craft, the more your ego fades. You are less consumed by what you, as an individual, want to obtain and more by what "we" can harness to perform a duty that is larger than yourself— making a difference on a grand scale, changing lives for the better, bringing hope when there appears to be little, saving the day when others don't think it can be salvaged, tapping into empathy, develop- ing others, performing at your strongest when things are bleak. As a good friend always said, be a supernova, illuminating the brightest light contagious to all who are watching.

Assuming a leadership role requires taking an oath to perform at your highest self with a nonwavering commitment. As we think about what it takes to execute effective care management programs and all of its complexities, sustainability and growth strategies can't be achieved without a true leader who can handle the proposition. Healthcare leaders must ensure members receive high-quality services throughout their healthcare continuum from requesting services, obtaining treatment in outpatient or inpatient entities, receiving proper advocacy and customized education with timely and thorough follow-up, delivering standardized operations aligned with state/ federal compliance mandates and leading practice methodologies, and meeting enterprise-wide metrics mapped to member safety and increased revenue.

People go to college to become doctors, engineers, project managers, human resource analysts, nurses, and computer programmers. In each discipline it was understood that an educational program provides the learnings necessary to perform these roles at a certain level of quality and competence. The same applies to leaders, and although there are natural elements, they need expansion and fine-tuning following a versatile working model.

Remember, start with self-awareness, understanding "you." Get help with this, if you haven't already, from a personal development coach. Understand how your personal influences from family or those individuals close to you can affect your ability to accept others from different cultures. Know before you act how you communicate and process information, what stresses you out, and what's most important to you.

I understand leaders must balance their responsibilities, focusing on the big picture without being distracted with granular efforts, but I learned through many years of leadership that you have to get into the weeds and spend a significant time there. If you are facing challenging operational gaps, don't worry about it today; time will lessen the blow as you steadily resolve things. You cannot appropriately assess what's going on in your operations and develop comprehensive solutions if you do not understand every phase of the member healthcare journey and what is supposed to happen from providers, your internal team, external vendors, and the member. Compliance standards and mandates set the framework for operational processes with associated policies, procedures, and workflows, and it is critical for leaders to understand them. Not doing so can lead to costly consequences. You have a compliance team, but your deep involvement is required. This is the most challenging phase as a leader, but the key is to stay focused. Don't get defeated, review operational documents, take additional trainings, participate in compliance webinars, and stay connected with other key experts, including health plan leaders, industry consultants, leading system technology vendors, human resource gurus, and data analysts.

Don't forget that your team is like an extended family. Focus on bonding. Build trust and integrity by getting to know who they are outside of work and at work. Many team members today feel a disconnect with leaders and forgotten, thinking they don't matter and are only workhorses. Spending a few minutes with them privately, allowing them to share their story, will do wonders. Let them get to know you too; bring them into your personal space with appropriate boundaries. Learn their work styles and preferences and require them to participate in a personality type indicator test. Refer to their results frequently, especially when determining how to communicate and support their performance.

Train your teams effectively. Most team members want to perform well with inherent values and standards, and it doesn't sit well with them when they feel they cannot perform their duties at a quality level or simply don't understand their role. Lack of training is a consistent challenge with some healthcare organizations, mentioned in staff surveys, exit interviews, polling, staff meetings, and one-to-one meetings. Developing an effective plan requires commitment; work with training experts, HR, and key team members to build engaging manuals, PowerPoints, modules, and cheat sheets aligned with policies, procedures, and enterprise-wide goals. Deliver trainings in large and small groups and offer various ways for them to learn, including classroom setting, focus groups, side-by-side observations, self-paced modules, and personal development courses. Remember that your team is diverse with different learning and communication preferences, originating from different generations, including baby boomers; Generations X, Y, and Z; and millennials, and a birth range from 1942 to 2000.

Most individuals want to grow, moving into other positions to meet specific goals, earning more money, becoming an expert, making an impression in the industry, receiving recognition, or pleasing those close to them. Propose customized career development plans; understand each team member's professional goals and the responsibilities they enjoy most. Evaluate their competency levels over time and provide recommendations on career paths most suitable to for them to succeed. Although a promotion is a popular request, offers are limited to positions available through your organization; be honest with your team members, but continue to encourage them to learn more skills aligned with their personality type. Show other ways they can utilize their newly learned skills to improve process flow, train peers, increase member satisfaction, and build strong rapport with cross-functional teams.

Learning never stops, especially in healthcare. The field is always changing, with constantly moving targets, advanced treatments, new health conditions and technology, and innovation occurring before we can fully adopt previous enhancements. Instead of taking it one day at a time, take it one hour at a time. Breathe. You've got this.

Leaders, we are the first line, standing in combat to tackle some of the most daunting efforts to protect and advocate for our community. Healthcare is a convoluted, complex, and evolving industry that many have attempted to improve yet came up short. We must learn from our past and stay committed to saving lives while representing integrity, honesty, and resilience and fostering healthy relationships to regain hope and trust to advance others' skills and build an enduring legacy.

When I saw the smile on my sister's face after helping her regain steady breathing as a child, I didn't know what my future would look like or what was required of me to care for others in the same way. Looking back as a seasoned professional with so many experiences and a blend of positive growth opportunities to stretch my abilities, I know the common denominator to my continued success is an infinite love and passion to help others. In our busy and competitive society, many of us are programmed to lead with our left brain, encompassing logic, analytical concepts, and intellectual thinking, but neglecting our right brain to foster emotions, intuition, creativity, and nurturing. Without equal use of both, we experience an imbalance.

Tap into this powerful space as you add to your leadership toolbox. Leading with compassion rewards with recognition, personal gratitude, and most importantly, a fulfilling life of giving back.

Appendix

Utilization Management Context

It's imperative for you as an industry expert to understand utilization management. UM is an objective process that uses an evidence-based criteria to evaluate requested healthcare services to make fair and timely determinations about all services requiring review for appropriateness during the member journey, resulting in an approval or denial. The criteria further includes the following:

- Collection and use of relevant clinical information, for example, H&P, progress notes, imaging study results, and mediations to make utilization management decisions

- Qualified health professionals to assess requests and make utilization management decisions. These clinicians are nurses and pharmacy technicians with the support of physicians who are licensed and qualified to make determinations.

- Alignment with state requirements and regulatory agencies standards/mandates instructing how to operate the UM department, including the Utilization Review Accreditation

Commission (URAC), the National Committee for Quality Assurance (NCQA), and the Centers for Medicare and Medicaid Services (CMS).

It is critical for industry experts to understand these regulatory agencies' standards/mandates to meet compliance. Missing this step will significantly impact operational delivery, resulting in penalties/sanctions and possible suspension or termination of the health plan to market plans across exchange, commercial, Medicare, and Medicaid lines of business. Not meeting the compliance requirements is seen as an industry trend and negatively affected several health plans across our nation.

NCQA accreditation requirements includes a combination of documented processes, reports, materials, records, files, and model of care for standards/mandates below.

Note: Recommend an industry expert to review technical NCQA accreditation specifications for more details; the requirements listed below are high level. Also, modifications are made annually, and information is up to date for the current year. Check for changes in future years.

- Program structure

- Clinical criteria for UM decisions

- Communication services

- Appropriate professionals

- Timeliness of UM decisions

- Clinical information

- Denial notices

- Policies for appeals

- Appropriate handling of appeals

- Evaluation of new technology

- Procedures for pharmaceutical management

- System controls

- Delegation of UM

URAC accreditation requirements include a combination of documented processes, policies, and job descriptions for standards/mandates below.

Note: Recommend an industry expert to review technical URAC accreditation specifications for more details; the requirements listed below are high level. Also, modifications are made annually, and information is up to date for the current year. Check for changes in future years.

- Review criteria requirements

  - Access to review staff

  - Review service communication and time frames

  - Review service disclosures

  - On-site review requirements

  - Limitations in use of nonclinical staff

  - Prereview screening staff oversight

  - Preview-review screening noncertifications

  - Initial clinical reviewer qualifications

  - Initial clinical reviewer resources

  - Initial clinical reviewer noncertifications

  - Peer clinical review cases

- Peer clinical reviewer qualifications

- Drug utilization management reviewer qualifications

- Prospective, concurrent, and retrospective drug utilization management

- Peer-to-peer conversation availability

- Peer-to-peer conversation alternate

- Prospective review time frames

- Retrospective review time frames

- Concurrent review time frames

- Certification decision notice and tracking

- Continued certification decision requirements

- Written notice of noncertification decisions and rationale

- Clinical rationale for noncertification requirements

- Prospective review patient safety

- Reversal of certification determinations

- Frequency of continued reviews

- Scope of review information

- Prospective and concurrent review determinations

- Retrospective review determinations

- Lack of information policy and procedures

- Noncertification appeals process

- Appeals process

- Appeal peer reviewer qualifications

- Drug utilization management appeals: reviewer

- Qualifications

- Reviewer attestation regarding credentials and knowledge

- Expedited appeal process time frame

- Standard appeal process time frame

- Written notice of upheld noncertifications

- Appeal record documentation

- Independent (external) review process

CARE MANAGEMENT AND COMPLIANCE CONTEXT

Care management is a team-based, member-centered approach designed to assist members and their support systems in managing medical conditions more effectively. It starts once the member seeks treatment and continues through all phases of inpatient and outpatient medical services. It encompasses care coordination activities needed to help manage a chronic illness.

It's imperative for you, as an industry expert, to understand care management program operations, ensuring members receive appropriate guidance, education, and quality services from both internal and external team members involved with member care. This will eliminate gaps in care and increase profitability. Some health plan care management programs include

- maternity,

- chronic care management,

- complex care,

- behavioral health,

- health advocacy,

- transplant,

- end-stage renal disease (ESRD),

- 24/7 nurse line, and

- cancer support.

Moreover, it is critical for industry experts to understand regulatory agencies' standards/mandates to meet care management program compliance similar to UM. Again, missing this step will significantly impact operational delivery, resulting in penalties/sanctions and possible suspension or termination of health plan to market plans across exchange, commercial, Medicare, and Medicaid lines of business. Not meeting the compliance requirements is seen as an industry trend and negatively affected several health plans across our nation.

NCQA accreditation and quality requirements include a combination of documented processes, reports, materials, records, files, and model of care for standards/mandates below.

Note: Recommend an industry expert to review technical NCQA accreditation specifications for more details; the requirements listed below are high level. Also, modifications are made annually, and the information is up to date for the current year. Check for changes in future years.

ACCREDITATION

Standards for Quality Management and Improvement

- Program structure and operations

- Health services contracting

- Continuity and coordination of medical care

- Continuity and coordination between medical care and behavioral healthcare

- Delegation of QI

Standards for Population Health Management

- PHM strategy

- Population identification

- Delivery system supports

- Wellness and prevention

- Complex case management

- Population health management impact

- Delegation of PHM

Standards for Utilization Management

- Program structure

- Clinical criteria for UM decisions

- Communication services

- Appropriate professionals

- Timeliness of UM decisions

- Clinical information

- Denial notices

- Policies for appeals

- Appropriate handling of appeals

- Evaluation of new technology

- Procedures for pharmaceutical management

- UM system controls

- Delegation of UM

Standards for Long-Term Services and Supports
- Core features

- Measuring and improving performance

- Care transitions

- Delegation of LTSS

Standards for Medicaid
- Medicaid benefits and services

- Practice guidelines

- Practitioner office site quality

- Privacy and confidentiality

- Care coordination

- Initial screening and assessment of members

- Quality assessment and performance improvement

- Informing members of services

- UM decisions about payment and services

- Grievances and appeals

- Continued coverage

- Information services for members

- Member communications

- Practitioner and provider directories

- Delegation of MED

Standards for Medicare Advantage

- Disenrollment practices

- ESRD enrollment/disenrollment

- Initial assessment "best effort"

- Advance directives

- Notification to practitioners regarding network decisions

- Credentialing criteria and performance monitoring for recredentialing

- Practitioner and provider participation

- Practitioner and provider network

- Contracts

- Appeals process for termination/suspension

- Conscience objection notice

- Direct access to practitioners

- Access to services

- Emergency services

- Standards for medical record documentation

- Quality improvement program

- Ensuring appropriate utilization

- Delegation of health plan standards

- QI program structure

- Program operations

- Continuity and coordination of medical care

- Continuity and coordination between medical care and behavioral healthcare

- Utilization program structure

- Clinical criteria for UM decisions

Standards for Special Needs Plans
- Enrollment verification

- Assessing and coordinating care

- Plan performance monitoring and evaluation of the model of care (MOC)

In addition, you as an industry expert should understand network management, credentialing and recredentialing, and member experience standards as well.

QUALITY—THE HEALTHCARE EFFECTIVENESS DATA AND INFORMATION SET (HEDIS)

One of the most important CMS strategic goals is to improve the quality of care and general health status for Medicare beneficiaries. Their strategy includes a partnership with NCQA, who developed quality targets called Healthcare Effectiveness Data and Information Set (HEDIS) to evaluate the performance of health plans, physicians, hospitals, and other providers. A subset of these measures are used for the Medicare population. Health plans can earn a star rating of 1 through 5; these ratings are driving improvements in Medicare quality with significant oversight.

HEDIS includes more than ninety measures across six domains of care:
- Effectiveness of care

- Access/availability of care

- Experience of care

- Utilization and risk-adjusted utilization

- Health plan descriptive information

- Measures reported using electronic clinical data systems

The CMS quality monitoring requirements include a combination of documented processes, reports, records, files, and model of care for standards/mandates below.

Note: Recommend an industry expert to review the CMS requirements for more details; the requirements listed below are high level. Also, modifications may occur, and information is up to date for the current year. Check for changes in future years.

HEALTH PLANS MUST FOCUS ON QUALITY IMPROVEMENT AREAS

- Chronic Care Improvement Program (CCIP) – Cover all non-special-needs coordinated care plans; health plan must be submitted by December 31 annually.

- Maternal and Infant Healthcare Quality – Preterm birth and low birth weight, with associated economic and social costs, are high in the United States; their impacts can be long lasting, particularly among the most vulnerable populations.

  → Improve the rate and content of postpartum visits.

  → Increase the use of effective methods of contraception among women in Medicaid and CHIP.

Health plans are required to provide maternity programs and coordinate with providers/vendors.

- Care of Acute and Chronic Conditions (Asthma) – Improve asthma control collaborative learning, reduce obesity by referrals to weight management programs, and collaborate with PCP, specialists, and weight management programs for BMI checks and care planning. Health plans are required to provide weight management programs and coordinate with providers/vendors.

- Behavioral Healthcare (Tobacco Cessation) – In comprehensive tobacco cessation programs, including quit line and counseling, health plans are required to provide the program.

- Dental and Oral Healthcare Initiative – A referral to a dentist is required for every child in accordance with the periodicity schedule set by a state. Provide at least emergency services for adults; a health plan can support coordination of care with participating providers.

- Preventive Care

  - Childhood Screening – Comprehensive health and developmental history, comprehensive unclothed physical exam, appropriate immunizations, laboratory tests (including lead toxicity screening), health education (anticipatory guidance including child development, healthy lifestyles, and accident and disease prevention).

  - Vaccines – Children vaccines covered by Medicaid; some adult vaccines are covered.

  - Outreach Tools – Living Well is a set of outreach and education materials that connects preventive care in the clinical setting with everyday life. The Living Well toolkit features customizable posters, fact sheets, social media posts, and strategies for getting the word out about Medicaid coverage of preventive services.

➡ Patient Safety – The Partnership for Patients brings together leaders of major hospitals, employers, physicians, nurses, and patient advocates along with state and federal governments in a shared effort to make hospital care safer, more reliable, and less costly.

➡ Keep patients from getting injured or sicker.

➡ Help patients heal without complication.

Health plans are required to report incidents and support care transitions.

- Long-Term Services and Support

- Improving care transitions between care settings is critical to improving individuals' quality of care and quality of life and their outcomes. Effective care transitions

    ➡ prevent medical errors,

    ➡ identify issues for early intervention,

    ➡ prevent unnecessary hospitalizations and readmissions,

    ➡ support consumers' preferences and choices, and

    ➡ avoid duplication of processes and efforts to more effectively utilize resources.

- The cross-agency Partnership for Patients initiative is decreasing hospital readmissions by improving care transitions and community-based care.

- Hospital engagement networks (HENs) are working with community providers to improve transitions.

- An aging and disability resource center provides information for states and community organizations that want to identify and access a range of home and community-based resources to make positive changes to their long-term services system, including home-based interventions.

- The Community-Based Care Transitions Program (CCTP), created by section 3026 of the Affordable Care Act, tests models for improving care transitions from the hospital to other settings and reducing readmissions for high-risk Medicare beneficiaries.

- The Money Follows the Person initiative assists states in their efforts to reduce reliance on institutional care while developing community-based long-term care opportunities.

- Medicare resources help caregivers manage varying issues and lead balanced, rewarding lives.

- Health plans need to evaluate if facilities and providers are participating and supporting communication/coordination with members.

SOCIAL DETERMINANTS OF HEALTH (SDOH)

Although HPs have long discovered social factors as primary drivers of health outcomes and been working for many years to address them, recently HPs, providers, and government agencies have sharpened their focus on addressing SDoH. This is due to mounting evidence that some of these initiatives are associated with improved health outcomes and reduced healthcare utilization; recent state and federal laws now require or encourage plans to coordinate with community and social support providers, and the growth and maturity of value-based care (VBC) provides a financial incentive, if not a financial imperative, to deliver better health outcomes by using resources more efficiently and effectively.

There is evidence that social factors are primary drivers of health outcomes. These factors include the following:

- Housing instability/homelessness – member unable to pay rent, living on the street in unsanitary conditions

- Food insecurity – member with diabetes admitted to hospital attributed to inability to afford nutritional foods

- Transportation – for example, delayed asthma medication changes related to member missing appointments because of not having a car and relatives not available to take member to appointments in a timely manner

- Education – member with no high school diploma, not able to obtain a decent-paying job to sustain adequate living conditions

- Utility needs – member not having enough money to pay gas, electric, and water bills, resulting in increased stress levels

- Interpersonal violence – member exposed to intentional violence, like an abusive parent, causing injury or harm

- Family support – member living with family members not engaged in member care plan who smoke in the home and cook unhealthy foods

- Employment and income – member unable to get or keep a job or gain steady income, resulting in inability to buy medications and medical supplies

HP care managers assess members for these factors during their initial care management outreach and document information in appropriate assessment and care plan, submitting referrals to internal programs and providers (nutritionists, wellness programs, community organizations, social workers, pharmacy rebate programs, etc.) to address gaps.

An industry trend of HPs tending to implement SDoH programs at scale without rigorous evidence of effect, rather than targeting interventions to specific patients and assessing their impact, has been identified. It's recommended to screen for and address SDoH, which should receive the same scrutiny as clinical interventions to diagnose and treat disease.

POPULATION HEALTH

Over the last five to seven years, there has been a rapid change in policy decision-making, payment structures, and provider alignment; they have shifted the focus from care provided and paid for at an individual level to managing and paying for healthcare services for a discrete or defined population called population health. Although health plans were already segmenting member populations by their contractual employer groups and community/geographic areas with targeted interventions, they have an increased focus on partnering with providers of accountable care organizations (ACO) and patient-centered medical home (PCMH) using assessments and other data sources like patient registries to guide annual risk stratification to appropriately manage groups with specific medical and social needs. HPs are also aiming to improve data sharing/information exchange that a provider may not have access to (e.g., pharmacy, ED reports, enrollment, program eligibility, gaps in care reports, claims, SDoH assessments, data from other providers), moving to an effective integrated approach.

Some initiatives that HPs are using are as follows:

- Pre-evaluation to determine if the provider meets the following:

  → General Medicaid and Medicare compliance – fraud, waste, and abuse compliance training; code of conduct training; exclusion check prior to hiring or contracting and, monthly thereafter, confirming that providers are not barred from Medicare or Medicaid programs; compliance work plan; policy and reporting that demonstrates the ability to fulfill the contract deliverables

  → Integrated governance and accountability requirements – active and integrated approach of clinical services as integrated model of care and achieving patient outcomes, incorporation of state and federal regulation that governs activities, advance electronic record technology system with proper safeguards and processes, implementation monitoring, and continuous improvement strategies and initiatives

  → Operational culture of excellence – hiring and developing a culture of high-caliber talent, high-quality leaders, and staff and associates who are well trained, which creates and build a team that focuses on customer service, team-based integrated care and continuous improvement, processes with real-time and up-to-date reflection of organizational and IT policies or workflows with job aids and quick training, and data that is meaningful, organized, and readily available to all team members

➡ A strong transition of care (TOC) program – structured approach to ensure coordinated care and continuity of care; member engagement and education utilizing a multilayered approach to interventions so that patients do not fall through the cracks

• Performing annual audits of providers based on key performance measures and evidence-based guidelines including

➡ NCQA, URAC, and CMS quality and quality improvement requirements;

➡ Agency for Healthcare Research and Quality (AHRQ) patient safety indicators associated with a provider;

➡ inpatient quality indicators;

➡ risk-adjusted measures of mortality, complications, and readmission;

➡ quality payment program (QPP) measures;

➡ non-QPP qualified clinical data registry (QCDR) measures;

➡ Consumer Assessment of Healthcare Providers and Systems (CAHPS) clinician and group survey; and

➡ The American Medical Association's Physician Consortium for Performance Improvement (PCPI) measures

Based on audit results, an HP may recommend corrective action, recommendations, or termination of contract if the provider fails to meet expectations by a specified time.

- Offering provider incentive programs giving providers bonuses for how well they perform member care related to quality and cost metrics

The overall goal for an HP and provider partnership is to provide member-centric, valued-based care in alignment with mandated regulatory agencies' quality standards to promote member well-being while sustaining or increasing profitability.

Resources

Federal Statutes

Implementation of the CMS Interoperability and Patient Access final rule and compliance with the ONC Twenty-First-Century Cures Act final rule—42 CFR Parts 431, 435, 438, 440, and 457:

§422.568, and an expedited procedure for situations in which applying the standard procedure could seriously jeopardize the enrollee's life, health, or ability to regain maximum function, in accordance with §§422.570 and 422.572.

Federal Integrated plan, beginning January 1, 2021, plans must comply with §§422.629 through 422.634 in lieu of §§422.566(c) and (d), 422.568, 422.570 and 422.572 with regard to the procedures for making determinations, including integrated organization determinations and integrated reconsiderations, on a standard and expedited basis.

Cited References: [63 FR 35067, June 26, 1998, as amended at 65 FR 40329, June 29, 2000; 68 FR 50858, Aug. 22, 2003; 70 FR 4739, Jan. 28, 2005; 75 FR 19812, Apr. 15, 2010; 75 FR 32859, June 10, 2010; 76 FR 21569, Apr. 15, 2011; 84 FR 15834, April 16, 2019]

Further Reading

https://www.ncqa.org/

https://www.urac.org/

https://www.cms.gov/

https://www.ahip.org/

https://www.medicaid.gov/

https://www.himss.org/

Altus ACE Readiness Preparation and Analysis for UMAG Clinical Integration.

Goleman, Daniel. *Emotional Intelligence.* New York: Random House, 2005.

Jain, Sachin H., and Pooja Chandrashekar. "Implementing a Targeted Approach to Social Determinants of Health Interventions." *Am J Manag Care* 26, no. 12 (2020): 502–4. https://doi.org/10.37765/ ajmc.2020.88537

Lee, Josh, and Jeff Burke. "Addressing the Social Determinants of Health for Medicare and Medicaid Enrollees," 2019. https://www2. deloitte.com

"Myers-Briggs Type Indicator (MBTI) | Official Myers-Briggs Personality Test." https://themyersbriggs.com

Newby, Timothy J., and Ashlyn Heide. "The Value of Mentoring." *Performance Improvement Quarterly* (1992).

CPSIA information can be obtained
at www.ICGtesting.com
Printed in the USA
JSHW031438160422
25022JS00008B/175